Presentation Design:
Don't Bore Me with PowerPoint
Second Edition

Sol Schneider

Australia · Canada · Mexico · Singapore · Spain · United Kingdom · United States

Presentation Design
Sol Schneider

Executive Editors:
Michele Baird, Maureen Staudt &
Michael Stranz

Project Development Manager:
Linda deStefano

Sr. Marketing Coordinators:
Lindsay Annett and Sara Mercurio

Production/Manufacturing Manager:
Donna M. Brown

Production Editorial Manager:
Dan Plofchan

Pre-Media Services Supervisor:
Becki Walker

Rights and Permissions Specialist:
Kalina Ingham Hintz

Cover Image
Getty Images*

The Adaptable Courseware Program
consists of products and additions to
existing Thomson products that are
produced from camera-ready copy.
Peer review, class testing, and
accuracy are primarily the responsibility
of the author(s).

Title Presentation Design
Author Sol Schneider

ISBN: 978-1-4266-3601-1
ISBN: 1-4266-3601-6

International Divisions List

Asia (Including India):
Thomson Learning
(a division of Thomson Asia Pte Ltd)
5 Shenton Way #01-01
UIC Building
Singapore 068808
Tel: (65) 6410-1200
Fax: (65) 6410-1208

Australia/New Zealand:
Thomson Learning Australia
102 Dodds Street
Southbank, Victoria 3006
Australia

Latin America:
Thomson Learning
Seneca 53
Colonia Polano
11560 Mexico, D.F., Mexico
Tel (525) 281-2906
Fax (525) 281-2656

Canada:
Thomson Nelson
1120 Birchmount Road
Toronto, Ontario
Canada M1K 5G4
Tel (416) 752-9100
Fax (416) 752-8102

UK/Europe/Middle East/Africa:
Thomson Learning
High Holborn House
50-51 Bedford Row
London, WC1R 4LS
United Kingdom
Tel 44 (020) 7067-2500
Fax 44 (020) 7067-2600

Spain (Includes Portugal):
Thomson Paraninfo
Calle Magallanes 25
28015 Madrid
España
Tel 34 (0)91 446-3350
Fax 34 (0)91 445-6218

Acknowledgements

My best friend's mother taught me this, "People should have their flowers while they're living." Mrs. Lowell Carter passed away recently but her friendship and that of her son, Dr. Steve Reames, have comforted me over the past 48 years.

My wife, Deborah Greene, brings her happiness with her wherever she goes. It may be why people seek her company. Debi has helped me to thrive when away from work. My friends at Congregation Beth Shalom of the Woodlands inspired me to learn Hebrew at age 60.

My wonderful friends on the faculty of SHSU- Dr. Cooper, Dr. Burris, Dr. Maguire, Judy Bennett, David Collins, Gary and Lisa, Dr. Jihuang Ji, Ken, Karon, Katherine, Judi, Svetlana, and Dr. Li-Jen Shannon have helped me to feel like I truly belonged here at SHSU. Thanks also to Natalia Fofanova for co-authoring and Julianne Peterson for inspiring the very first edition.

Medical Doctors Mahesh Ramchandani, Milton Klein, David Ficklen, Stephen Sims, and Anisa Ghopolani, M.D., helped me survive to enjoy the intellectual satisfaction of revising this book.

To all of these wonderful, inspiring, generous people, I am grateful.

--Solomon Schneider, M.S., Instructional Technology

Sam Houston State University* Computing Sciences Dept. Huntsville, Texas 77341-2090

*A member of the Texas State University System

5 Menu Time Savers for MS Office© 2007 7

Overview: Quick Access Menu & Ribbon 8

Create A New Presentation 9

Concept Map – Initial Design Choices 10

Rip Out Test 1 12

Getting Started With Text..12

Text Placeholders- Map 13

Rip Out Test 2 14

Placeholders 14

Insert New Slides*- 15

Insert New Slides In Ppt © 2007 16

Rip Out Test 3 17

Shortcuts, Templates 17

Using Bulleted Text Effectively 19

Four, not more 19

7 +/- 2 Limit 19

Rip Out Test 4 20

Bullets 20

Choosing Bulleted Lists 20

4 Reasons to fill in a title placeholder 21

Rip Out Test 5 23

Layouts 23

Do We Use Design Templates? No. 24

Three Sample Templates from MS PPT© 2003 24

Edit Text Placeholders..26

Reshape Title Place Holders..26

Adding Color to Text Placeholders...27

Format, FonT Color = Control + "T" 28

Change font color in Powerpoint© 2007 29

Change Background Color in Ppt© 2007 29

Wasted Space In Text Placeholders 31

Even out the white space 31

Learning From Cognitive Psychology 32

Selective Perception and the Sensory Stores..32

Designing for Selective Perception 32

Limits on Short Term Memory...32

Rip Out Test 6 33

Sensory Store Memory...33

Rehearsal means creating associations 34

Designing for Bulleted Text 34

Limited capacity- 34

Rip Out Test 7 35
Capacity 35
Designing for Limited Capacity - Chunking 36
Long Term Memory 36
Implications for designers- 37

On the Master Slide 37
Set the Title Placeholder Case 37
A Highly Readable Font 39
Animate a Master Slide Bullet Box 40

Assignment 1: Text Placeholders 41

Locate RELEVANT images 45

Five principles for choice of font: 47
Wide Kerning (True Type) 47
Size 28 Points 49
Plain, Sans Serif Fonts 51
Six special effects 53
Five Text Design Decisions - Review 54
Open Book Test 1 55

Summary- 6 steps that make a slide a minute 56
30 Slides In 30 Minutes Concept Map 57
Choose the Right Tool 58
First Pass: Create New Slides 59
Second Pass: Make Bullets 59
Troubleshooting Tip...59

MS PPT 2007© Keyboard Shortcuts 61

Designing Slide Titles 61
Information Organizer...61
Describes Contents..61
Never animate title placeholders 62
Blank slide, blank mind 62
Open-Book Test 2 Placeholders...63

Custom Animation 64
AVOID "animation schemes" 64
CHOOSE "Slide show, custom animation" 64
Animation Sequence: Title, Photo, Text 65
Animate Text – Basic category; very fast 67
Animating a Bulleted Box 68
Troubleshooting Multiple Bullets...68
To remove animations 69

Animating graphics 70

Color, Font, Animatiom- Concept Map 70

Speed- Very Fast, Fast, Lost the Audience...71
Animating Photos, Embedding Camera Sound 71
Embed sound in a graphic-2 73

Organization of Effect Options, Sounds 74
Embed our voice in a photograph 74
Embed internet sound effects in a photograph 76
Selected animation effects...76
Open Book Test 3-Animation Design 77

SOUNDS 78
Change 2003 default settings 78
Where do sound files belong? 79
Map: Images & (Embedded) Sounds 79
Embedding sounds in 4 steps 80
Insert, Media Clips, Sound, Record Sound - PPT© 2007 80
PPT prerecorded sounds. 83
Internet sounds...84
Findsounds.com..84
Slide Show, Record Narration 87
Five Parts to Recording a Narration. 87
Windows Sound Recorder®. 88
Microphone and recording tips 89
Summary of 6 ways to add sound to PPT 90

Photos & the old Picture Toolbar 92
OPTIMIZING PHOTO BRIGHTNESS 95
Where to look..95
screen prints 96
photographs & effectiveness 96
Instantly zoom in and out...97
Do photos cure boredom? 97
Order of appearance 97
title, picture, text...97
Silence the bullets!...98

Graphics 99

The Draw Menu Became 100
Format Menu, ARRANGE Tab Heading 100
Transparent fill color PPT© 2007 103
Rotate or Flip..105
Align or Distribute 105
Grid & Guides...106
The Grid & Guides Dialog Box 107
Snap to grid 107
Shift-Click & Group, Ungroup...108

Assignment 2 – Guess "Who Am I?" 109

Assignment 3: Spy Voices 110

    Grading Rubric: Spy Voices.ppt 111

Assignment 4: Stamped Envelope 112

Link to video clips on the web 113

    Linking a photo to a video on the web- 115

    Copying and Pasting a Relevant Image - 116

    Use the Text tool on the Draw Tool Bar 117

    Format the First Concept Map Textbox 118

    Changing Hypertext Default Colors 120

Maximize Effectiveness 122

    The Nightly News 122

    Analogy 123

    Spaced Repetition 123

    Sounds 123

    Rehearse 124

Using Open Office 2.0 Impress 124

Color in Open Office Impress 130

    Color Contrast 130

Immediate Feedback on Open Book Test 1 134

Immediate feedback on Open Book Test 2 134

Immediate feedback Open Book Test 3 135

    More Questions 136

Concept Maps

To minimize text and make the organization of our topics transparent, we use strategies from cognitive psychology, the study of how people reason, learn, and solve problems. The diagram below is a cognitive tool known as a Concept Map. It satisfies the same needs as a roadmap in your car.

Time spent studying the few phrases of a Concept Map is spent effectively. Brevity makes slide shows more powerful (effective) and interesting. This book teaches cognitive strategies and tools plus what to click in the user interface and why.

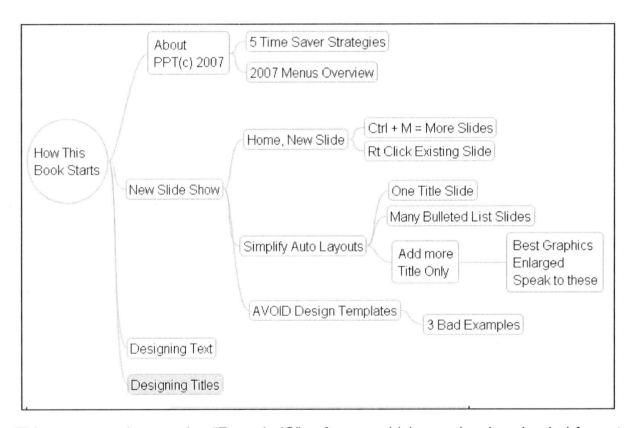

This map was drawn using "Freemind©" software, which may be downloaded free at PCWORLD.com. Browsing the Map lets us link the key concepts meaningfully.

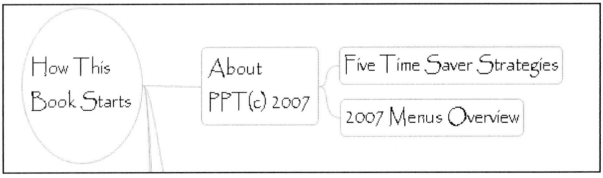

5 Menu Time Savers for MS Office© 2007

We offer five tips for playing hide-and-seek with the many new choices in Powerpoint© 2007. From most time saved to least:

1) Keyboard shortcut combinations from Powerpoint© 2003, called hotkeys, still work, saving the most time. For example, Ctrl + M is still "More slides."
2) Right clicking any object shows a useful "context sensitive" or shortcut menu.
3) The new menu choice "Home" holds miscellaneous-but-frequently-used commands. "Home" often has exactly what the right click menu is missing. Return to "Home" between navigation adventures.
4) The Function 1 key (F1) starts the Help menu. Rest the pointer on a Ribbon command. A ScreenTip tells what that command does. If you press F1 key you get more information targeting that specific command.
5) Download and leave open a MS help document that cross-references where to find 2003 commands in 2007 software. It is an Excel file whose numerous bottom tab headings are the endangered 2003 menu choices.

Type into Google's Search box the phrase "Locations of 2003 commands in PowerPoint 2007." You will quickly find the site http://office.microsoft.com/en-us/powerpoint/HA101490761033.aspx?pid=CH100668131033

The Excel file below1 comes from that cross-reference help file. It shows View, Header & Footer, was changed to Insert, Text, Header & Footer. The navigation buttons on the bottom left will display the 41 tab headings as needed.

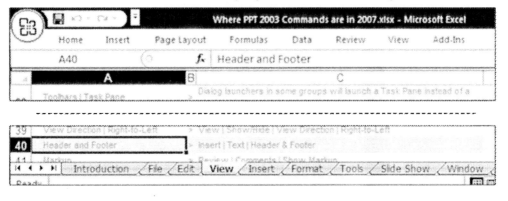

---

1 The Excel© Screen Print was retrieved from: http://office.microsoft.com/en-us/powerpoint/HA101490761033.aspx?pid=CH100668131033

Overview: Quick Access Menu & Ribbon

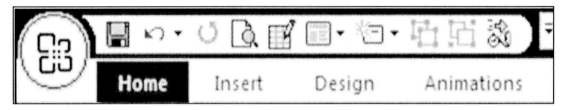

The **"Quick Access (QUACK!) Tool Bar"** occupies the top-most line in the left corner of the screen print above. It resembles the old Title Bar.

The File menu is now a round Office button with a clover leaf pattern done in the four familiar Google colors: red, yellow, green, blue. It is in the top left corner.

The **Quick Access (QUACK!) Menu Bar** is the old Menu Bar now context sensitive – what line two on the Ribbon reveals depends on what is selected.
The Ribbon will expand or hide when a menu word is double clicked.

The phrase "Picture Tools" is shown at the upper right of the QA Tool Bar because a picture was selected before the screen print was captured. Ribbon buttons related to pictures will appear as long as the picture stays selected.

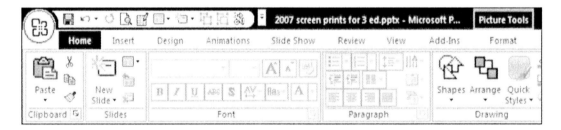

The Ribbon holds task-related toolbar buttons, grouped by **tab headings** beneath the Ribbon such as Clipboard, Slides, & Font. Above the Ribbon the revised menu bar resides. Clicking the Format menu choice above the Ribbon brings picture tools into view because a picture had recently been selected.

On the QA Menu Bar select the menu choice "Home." The Ribbon changes. The "Slides" Tab Heading is now the second from the left. **Home** holds highly probable next-click candidates not found on the right-click menu. **Home** Ribbon buttons come from widely different 2003 menu categories.

Tab headings (Clipboard, Slides, and Font above) appear under the Ribbon. Tab headings group related Ribbon buttons by function.

Create A New Presentation

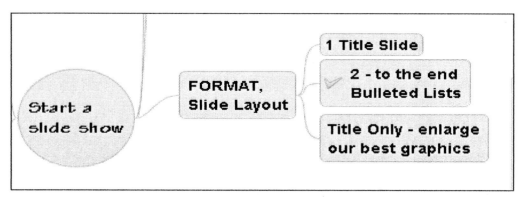

We start the software program and save the new project with a descriptive filename in two relevant locations: primary and backup.

The first two choices we make are:

1) Whether to start with a design template (we won't) and then

2) What type of new slide Auto Layouts we will insert (usually a bulleted list, for good reasons).

Selecting a design template was once thought to speed productivity by not having to think about formatting decisions. Today it takes so much time to preview the many design templates that it no longer serves that purpose.

Choose a "Blank New Presentation." Most existing templates have unwise color schemes that make it hard to read the text. Avoiding them entirely is a public service for your audience. Fill out the initial Title Slide then insert new slides.

Beneath the New Slide button on the Home Ribbon Menu (not on the Insert menu), the words "New Slide" next to a down-arrow symbol signify a drop down list box. That list box has options including the Slide Layout pattern. Use it to change the default Auto Layout choice of the New Slide button on the Ribbon when a change is needed. Now we can add some slides.

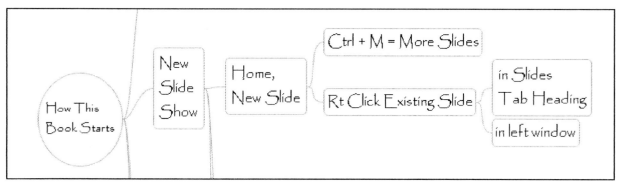

Control + M is the keyboard shortcut for More Slides; it also works in Open Office 2.0 Impress software and Star Office 8.0 Impress, two excellent free presentation programs.

We select an Auto Layout for the new slides next.

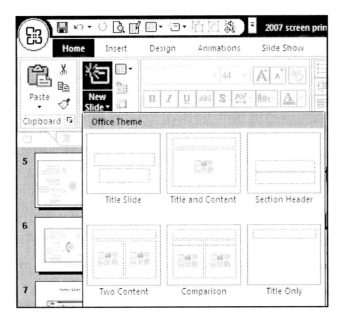

---Home, New Slide in PPT© 2007---

Click the Home ribbon menu choice to see New Slide options for Slide Layouts. Expect to use one Title Slide. Nearly all the other slides will be Title and Content (i.e., Single Bulleted List).

If a bulleted list slide has custom animation to reveal one point at a time it prevents a cluttered screen or cognitive overload. Cognitive psychologists like that approach.

Title Only slides show our best graphics, enlarged, with just a label (Title) at the top.

Using more Title Only slides is the wave of the future. It eliminates reading aloud the words on the slide (there is only a title).

Concept Map – Initial Design Choices

The diagram below is a Concept Map. If read counterclockwise, in the direction suggested by the curved arrow, it is also a flow chart. It diagrams choices to make when creating a presentation. Connecting lines show how all 25 phrases link to each other and to the main topic. The sequence flows from the top left. Concept Maps are learning roadmaps.

Sprinkled throughout this book are self quizzes which reinforce the material. Your instructor may assign the short quizzes for a grade.

This Concept Map was drawn using "Freemind©" software, which may be downloaded free at PCWORLD.com.

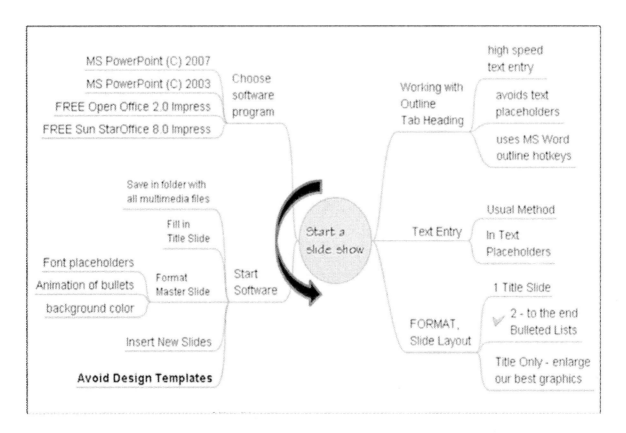

Choices that face us when we start a new slide show include what kinds of slide layouts to pick for new slides. The choice is pretty simple. The default choice is Title and Text (a single bulleted list). It is ideal for most slides for valid cognitive psychology reasons. PPT©2007 touts the all-in-one placeholders but older versions also would let users insert multimedia without special placeholders.

Most texts ignore the choice of where to type the text of a new presentation. Most novices type in the text placeholders, since after all, that's what they're for, right? This book takes the space to show how bypassing the text placeholders shaves several **hours** off the typical development time. The Concept Map above reveals the secret.

Rip Out Test 1

"Start a Show" Map

Getting Started With Text

Study the Concept Map above then **print** the letter of the best answers to these questions in the **left margin** or the blank line provided.

1. What other files must be saved in the same folder as a presentation?
    a. Pictures and drawings
    b. Sounds and music
    c. Links to web sites visited
2. What step must we do to avoid having to choose among Design Templates?
    a. Insert New Slide
    b. New Blank Presentation
    c. Format Master Slide
    d. Format Slide Layouts
3. Nearly all slides we insert will have the Slide Layout called ___?
    a. Title   b. Title & Text (a single bulleted list)
    c. Title Only (for large graphics)   d. Blank
4. The fastest way to get most the text into a presentation is
    a. Type it into Text Placeholders - determined by the Slide Layout.
    b. Type it into the Outline View – a tab heading in the left window in Normal view.
    c. Type it in Slide Sorter view.
5. A Concept Map can show
    a. How topics are related to each other
    b. How a presentation flows (its sequence)
    c. Prerequisite steps or knowledge
    d. All of the above.
6. (True / False) One full-featured presentation program that is free is named "Open Office Impress." _____
7. (True / False) A new presentation gives us all the slides we would ever hope to use. _____ ?
8. (True / False) Every phrase on the first Concept Map above can be traced back to "Starting a Slide Show." _____
9. (Short Answer) Which of the Slide Layout choices should we try to use **more**, if we trust the learning psychologists who say, "Research shows we must use less text and more graphics." _____.

Text Placeholders- Map

About Ninety percent of a presentation's message is transmitted by words- even in the best multimedia shows. Text must be easy to read and to recall. Our voice and sounds we play must be audible. If not? All the time we invest in the presentation will be wasted. Novices mistakenly believe any text a computer creates and prints is legible. We believe default settings for sounds, fonts, and colors can never be trusted.

Study the Concept Map below (PPT Basics) about entering text. Predict the order of the major ideas coming next. Concept Maps speed mastery.

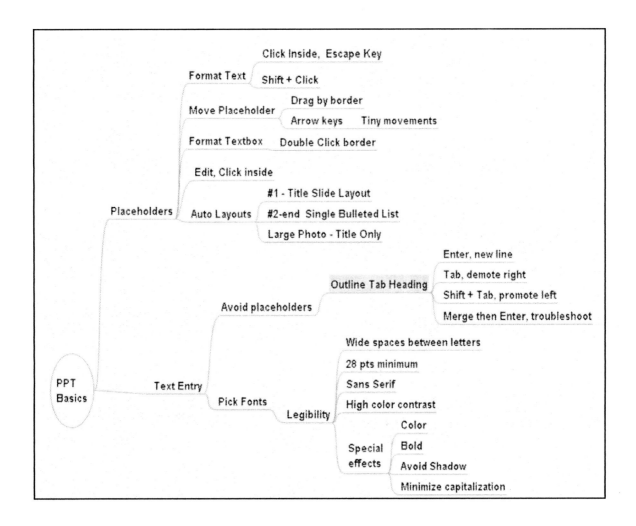

PPT Basics- What follows is about how to design text: how to work within textboxes, pick the three best Auto Layouts, select highly readable fonts, and how to skip text placeholders entirely, to speed text entry. A brief quiz will follow.

Rip Out Test 2

Powerpoint Basics Map

Placeholders

Study the previous concept map then write the letter of the best answers to these questions in the left margin.

1. How should we select a placeholder when we need to **edit** its content?
    a. Shift + Click the box
    b. Click inside the box
    c. Click inside the box and hit the Escape key.
    d. Double click its border.
2. How should we select a placeholder when we need to **format** its text?
    a. Shift + Click the box
    b. Draw a selection rectangle larger than the textbox.
    c. Click inside the box and hit the Escape key.
    d. All of the above.
3. How can we **move** a text placeholder precisely, for best control?
    a. Click on the border of the box then drag with the mouse.
    b. Click inside the textbox then drag anywhere with the mouse.
    c. Click inside the box & hit "Escape" then use keyboard arrow navigation keys.
    d. Select a placeholder and hit the right or left arrow buttons on the tool bar.
    e. Both a. and also c.
4. A Blank new presentation starts with a "Title" Auto Layout. The default "Auto Layout" style widely used for slide 2 through the end is:
    a. Title only (no subtitle box)
    b. Single bulleted list
    c. Blank (no title box)
    d. Double bulleted list
5. It is true that the fastest method of presentation text-entry avoids placeholders. Instead, the text of a new presentation ought to be typed where?
    a. Into text placeholders
    b. Into Slides, which is a tab heading in the left pane.
    c. Into Outline, which is a tab heading in the left pane.
    d. Into Slide Sorter View
6. The **most legible** (readable) font face for a new presentation ought to have
    a. Low color contrast
    b. Shadow special effect
    c. Wide spaces between the letters
    d. A Serif font face

Undo Mistakes with Ctrl + Z

The most valuable keyboard combination or shortcut to know is Control + Z. It undoes commands (mistakes).

Use two hands for keyboard combinations. It keeps the "pinky" finger from rising up off the Control key. Hold down the control key ("CTRL"). Then with one finger of the other hand, tap "Z" once. There are "CTRL" keys on both sides of the space bar. Here is a memory aid: to reverse the last command, recall the last letter of the alphabet. One can reverse a maximum of 16 previous commands. Are there exceptions? Two menu commands that may not be reversed are file, save and file, print.

Insert New Slides*-

In PPT © 2003 and OO Impress 2.0

*We abbreviate PowerPoint© as PPT©, & Open Office as O.O. after this.

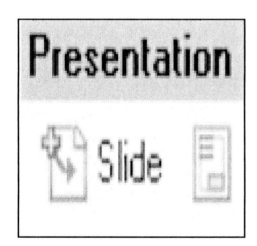

With PPT© 2003 open, insert a new slide by using the keyboard shortcut, **Ctrl + M**. for "More slides."

Most presentation software lists "**Slide**" as a choice under **INSERT** on the menu bar.

The "insert slide" shortcut in **O.O. Impress** is the "Presentation toolbar" button shown on the left. The free program Impress is stricter about placing the cursor inside the existing text of a placeholder to edit the object.

Default Auto Layout- All presentation software inserts new slides with a title placeholder and a bulleted text box by default. The Auto Layout name for the default bulleted text look is "Title and Text" in MS PPT© 2003, and is called "Title, Text" in O.O. Impress. PowerPoint© 2007 updates the default to the last Auto Layout chosen.

Cognitive-science- Defaulting to this bulleted text format is effective for cognitive-science reasons. Technological facts are learned fastest in the form of lists and comparison tables, slowest when presented as paragraph-formatted text. We must apply Custom Animation to most bulleted lists to show to the audience only one bullet at a time. Relieve the audience of deciphering a cluttered slide. Custom animation of bulleted lists prevents cognitive overload. It boosts retention by audience members.

Insert New Slides In Ppt © 2007

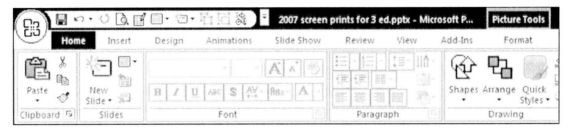

Notice that the largest, most prominent toolbar button on the Slides tab heading under the Ribbon is the New Slide button. This choice is located on the Homes menu, not the Insert menu choice above the Ribbon.

The quickest way to get a new slide is Control + M. Next fastest is if the View selected is Normal View, right click on a slide in the left window (the Slides Tab) and pick New Slide from the context sensitive menu. Third fastest is click the Ribbon menu choice Home as shown by the Screen Print above, and click the button New Slide.

The act of choosing the New Slide toolbar button inserts a slide with the same Layout as the last slide the user entered in PowerPoint© 2007; it previously defaulted to the bulleted list species of Auto Layout.

Beneath the New Slide button on the Ribbon, the words "New Slide" next to a down-arrow symbol signify a drop down list box. That drop down box has options including the Slide Layout pattern. Use it to change the default choice of the New Slide Tool Bar button.

On the Quick Access Menu Bar in MS PowerPoint© 2007, click the "VIEW" choice. On the leftmost edge of the Ribbon, the first ribbon button is now labeled "NORMAL." Push the Normal View button.

Once in Normal View, right-click any slide shown in the left Slides tab heading and choose New Slide from the right click menu, or, just hit the Enter Key.

The View Ribbon with the Normal button selected on the Ribbon Tool Bar.

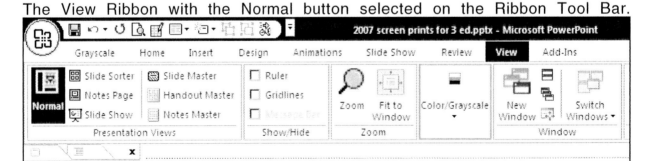

Images can be inserted without a special placeholder. Knowing this fact prevents wasting time on a bewildering array of little needed choices.

Rip Out Test 3

Undo Command

Shortcuts, Templates

Print Your Name (& class time or section number.) Score __ _ out of ___total

Write the letter of the best answers to these questions in the left margin.

1. What keyboard shortcut reverses or undoes our last PPT command?
     a. Ctrl + R   b. Ctrl + U   c. Ctrl + Z   d. Escape key
2. How many (maximum) commands can we cancel in PPT?
     a. 2   b. 4   c. 8   d. 16
3. We can NOT cancel which two Menu commands in PPT?
     a. Delete and Insert
     b. Save and Print
     c. Insert Reference and Insert Bookmark
     d. Draw, Group and Draw, Rotate, Flip
4. Which hand should we use for keyboard shortcuts?
     a. Left hand   b. Right hand   c. Either one   d. Both left and right
5. When we click inside a text placeholder it is selected:
     a. Slanted border lines
     b. Checkered lines
     c. For moving
     d. For total replacement
6. The best MS Design Template© to use is
     a. A template with medium shades
     b. One that has artwork on every slide
     c. One with artistic "shadow" font
     d. Don't use a MS Design Template©.

When we click in a text placeholder, we have two choices:

1) To type inside the placeholder to edit it, or

2) To select the whole textbox to be moved or formatted (like "edit, select all").

To Move or Format –

Choose VIEW, NORMAL in MS PowerPoint© 2003 or 2007. In O.O. Impress select the Normal tab heading in the central editing window.

Text Placeholder words ("Click here" etc.) are only hints that do not print. To move or reposition a text placeholder select it "all," with green resizing handles in Impress, or with a checkered border pattern in MS PPT© 2003, or a solid line in MS PPT© 2007.

Put the placeholder in the general neighborhood using the mouse. Fine tune its placement with arrow keys. Arrow keys move an object 1/12 of an inch with each tap.

To Edit or Type –

Click the pointer in the center of an unused placeholder right in the middle of the "Click to add title (or text)" hint. Notice now the border is made up of slanted or diagonal lines in both Impress and MS PPT©2003. In MS PPT©2007 a placeholder selected for editing has a dashed border line instead of a solid line. Click once on any of the borders instead, and it will be selected-all for moving not for editing.

> Text selected for editing- slanted border and green squares for resizing handles - Impress

A difference in the look of "selected-all" placeholders is that OO Impress has all green squares for resizing handles instead of white circles.

Browser Settings 2

PPT 2007

Selected-All is a solid line while Editing is a thin solid line border.

Selected for editing, MS PPT© 2007 has a dashed line, with round resizing handles in the corners, and square handles on the centers of the sides.

Use corner circles to resize boxes leaving them free of distortion. The tiny squares are best for cropping pictures, not resizing.

"Selected-all" - Some users hold the shift key down with the left hand and at the same time left-click the mouse button on the text placeholder. They are known as "shift clickers" but are not really cowboys. Shift + click selects placeholders "all," with a checkered border pattern (PPT© 2003) or a solid line (PPT© 2007).

A different "select-all" method is to **click inside the text placeholder** between words, **then hit the "escape" key** in the upper left corner of a keyboard.

The next slide in MS PPT© 2003 illustrates switching selections from edit mode to move/format mode- click inside the box and hit the "Escape" key.

18

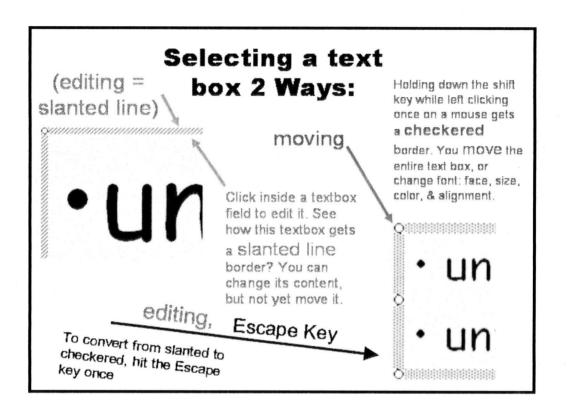

Using Bulleted Text Effectively

Autolayouts Auto layouts give slide shows a uniform, consistent look. Bulleted List Layouts can be enhanced by using the findings from cognitive psychology. With a few decisions we can convert material that would have been boring due to being hard to read and hard to comprehend, and we may make it easy to grasp and thus entertaining.

Large Font- Experienced presenters know bulleted text should be **at least 28+ points.** Large font drives brevity, and brevity creates clarity of meaning. Large font is also easier to read.

Four, not more - Limit slides to **four bulleted items maximum.** We know from cognitive psychologists who study learning that audiences won't remember long lists. Four bullets have 8 or more key words. The average person can only hear seven plus or minus two keywords before they begin forgetting.

Observe the eyes of others in an audience. Six bullets on one slide is two too many. See their eyes quit following when the fifth bullet appears. One way to avoid brain death from bullets (boredom) is to limit slides to four bullets.

7 +/- 2 Limit – The average person holds only seven plus or minus two facts or phrases in their "sensory store" (a tape recorder in the brain). **If more data is immediately presented, recent data is forgotten to hear what is new. This is called cognitive overload by learning theory psychologists.** Clearly, four bulleted text items hold at least seven things to think about. Stop at four bullets.

Making the font size 28+ points makes it hard to exceed four bullets.

Rip Out Test 4

Placeholders

Bullets

Print Your Name (& class time or section number.)
Score __ _ out of ___total

Print the letter of the best answers to these questions in the **left margin**.

1. If a text placeholder is selected for editing, then formatting changes are selected, what appears in the new format?
   a. Pictures and drawings
   b. All the text in the placeholder
   c. Text following the insertion point.
2. If a text placeholder is selected for editing, then we drag the border of the placeholder?
   a. The text placeholder moves.
   b. The height or width of the box changes
3. (True/False) The more information on a slide the shorter the presentation, and the more powerful it is.
4. Bulleted text boxes have been popular in business presentations because
   a. They help induce sleep.
   b. If animated correctly they improve audience recall.
   c. They encourage using key phrases instead of long sentences.
   d. The motion of flying bullets focuses attention when needed.
5. Bulleted list boxes should be limited to
   a. Three lines b. Six lines c. Four bullet items d. Six bullet items
6. Bulleted list boxes are widely used today by presenters mostly due to
   a. Habit & Tradition
   b. Proven effectiveness
   c. Attention grabbing animation schemes
7. (True/False) Making bulleted text at least 28 points prevents clutter.

Choosing Bulleted Lists

"Title Slide" Autolayout

The slide layout called "Title Slide" is good for the first slide. Increase the subtitle text to at least 28 points. Use it to announce a unique section within a show.

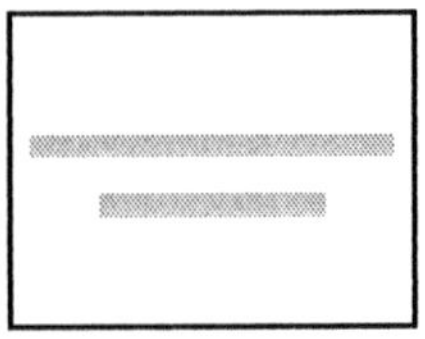

Title

Bulleted Lists Autolayout

Title & Text

These have "Title and Text" Autolayouts. Don't hesitate to make bulleted lists. Technical writing experts say showing technical information as lists and tables is more effective than displaying it in paragraph form. Animating the bullets properly prevents cluttered slides and boosts audience recall.

"Title and Text" autolayouts are used most, then slide layouts with charts and tables. The screen print above shows 3 parts of nearly every slide 1) title 2) graphic images 3) bulleted text.

The other 25 variations of Slide Layouts are safely ignored! Following are notes about less frequently needed autolayout choices.

"Title Only" Autolayouts –

Title Only

A title placeholder and much space for images. This is a great layout because of what it lacks- bulleted text. Choose it to speak longest to your very best visual examples; the audience prefers you not read to them.

Avoid "Blank" Autolayout

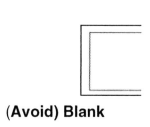

(Avoid) Blank

The worst auto layout is called the "Blank Slide." It has no placeholder for a title or for body text. **Even when we think we need no title, usually we still need one.**

4 Reasons to fill in a title placeholder

1) Titles are advance organizers and **using titles boosts recall**.
2) Printing the text of a show as an outline would make little sense.
3) Make titles if automatic Preview and Summary slides in Slide Sorter View are desired. Agenda slides use those features.
4) Hypertext links are easier to do if we have slide titles.

If we don't want a title to be visible, make the font color the same as the slide background and the title vanishes from sight. We can still read such hidden titles in the Outline Tab on the left windowpane, and in a Hyperlink dialog box.

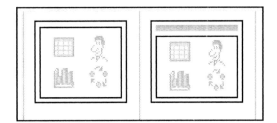

Compare these two autolayouts.

What makes the one on the right better?

{The title bar in gray on the right makes it better.}

To display tables, try doing the entire table formatting work in MS Word or O.O. Write, and pasting that into MS PPT©2007 as a finished object. PPT© table auto formats are faster, but pasted tables from MS Word can be formatted fancier in less time.

Not everyone needs all the autolayouts. The basic three are the title (for slide one), text and title, which is a bulleted list (for nearly all slides), and title only for large photos. Avoid the BLANK layout.

Rip Out Test 5

Placeholders

Layouts

Print Your Name (& class time or section number.)
Score ___ _ out of ___total

Print the letter of the best answers to these questions in the **left margin**.

1. A slide show needs only one ___ Autolayout?
   a. Title Only
   b. Title & Text
   c. Title
   d. Blank

2. The most unnecessary, unusable Autolayout is __?
   a. Title Only
   b. Title & Text
   c. Title
   d. Blank

3. (True/False) The more large photos, and the fewer words, as on a Title Only Autolayout, the more powerful the presentation is.

4. Bulleted text boxes have been popular in business presentations because
   a. They help induce sleep.
   b. If animated correctly they improve audience recall.
   c. They encourage using key phrases instead of long sentences.
   d. The motion of flying bullets focuses attention when needed.

5. (True/False) Importing a table from MS Word into Powerpoint© can be done without an autolayout field specially designed for tables.

6. Which statement below does NOT apply to using Title Placeholders?
   a. Titles are advance organizers
   b. Using titles boosts recall.
   c. Titles may be omitted
   d. Titles must be descriptive.

Do We Use Design Templates? No.

When we open a new MS PPT© file, we always skip the tempting choice "design template" and instead pick "New, Blank Presentation." MS Design Templates are typically ugly and illegible; we can do more interesting work starting from a blank presentation. Poor text and color defaults in existing templates bore an audience.

Three Sample Templates from MS PPT© 2003

Study these examples to find fault with readability. Then let's compare our defect lists…(Max)

Example 2 Wasted Space

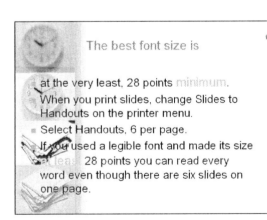

Can we read the slide on the left easily? Cover it up and ask what it said.

Any audience asked to struggle to read slides will not do so. It is up to the designer to make text easy to read.

The template (left) wasted our usable slide area with a large pattern that left little space for anything else. None of the 2005 design templates (or 2003) are works of art.

Example 3 – Streaks

Ex. 3 has a streaked background mixing light and dark. No font color exists that is legible against this background.

30 million people complain daily about boredom at slide shows. Would we recommend a movie to our friends if we could not see the characters?

The excursion into example templates was to prove anyone can find obvious flaws in MS Design Templates. Without the proof we might forget the advice to ...

A Blank New Presentation Needs

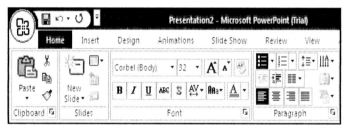

MS Powerpoint© 2007

The circular button with the cloverleaf design (Windows Logo) is the **Office** button, It replaces the file menu.

Open the Office (The FILE) button and choose NEW, BLANK PRESENTATION.

The Screen Print on the left is from Powerpoint©2007.

It has always been faster to start with File, New, Blank Presentation.

A recurring problem is the number of new template choices, though templates were once believed to speed starting new slide shows

As in earlier versions, the two "looks" that did not make it into the templates were "legible" and "easy to read." Nothing unmasks a novice like a template that obscures text.

Start with a blank New Presentation instead of an existing MS Design Template.

Edit Text Placeholders

The example below shows a slide's title placeholder centered across the top with an image that cannot fill the wasted space without obscuring text. Wasted space below the image can be reapplied, making the text larger. Reshaping a text placeholder is done on selected slides but not the Slide Master. Drag the white circles along the border of text boxes. They are called resizing handles.

Reshape Title Place Holders

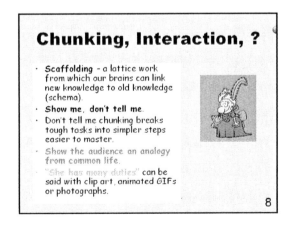

No rule says titles have to stretch symmetrically all the way across the top of a slide.

Reshape selected Title place holders by dragging the white circles (called resizing handles). Some textboxes made narrower line break differently creating more space to enlarge graphics.

Titles should be larger than body text which in turn should be > 28 points.

The example below shows the title of the slide above, both moved and reshaped, to make it break into three lines. The animated gif can now be enlarged.

The bulleted text box was stretched upward and automatically became a larger font size.

Placing images in a different spot may prevent audience sleepiness.

Remember, audience interaction has much more effect on boredom than any factor we can manipulate in designing a show.

Adding Color to Text Placeholders

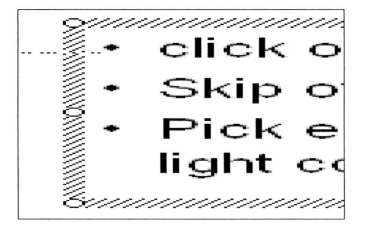

Double click the border of a text placeholder to add a fill color or a border line.

The defaults are "No fill" and "No line." Hence, text boxes appear invisible or seamless.

To select a fill color of a text box choose the opposite shade (bright / dark) to the font color. For the placeholder on our left, use a very light fill color inside the text box because the font is dark.

The white circles along the border in the (left) slide are named resizing handles.

Dragging a resizing handle to the textbox center shrinks it. Dragging away from the center enlarges it.

Resizing by a corner handle preserves the object's proportion if it is a picture. Dragging any other resizing handle distorts a picture.

Format, FonT Color = Control + "T"

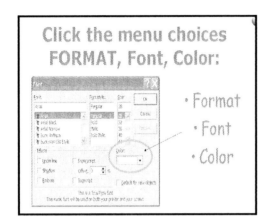

Click the menu choices
FORMAT, Font, Color:

- Format
- Font
- Color

Step 1: Select a text box so it has a checkered border.

Step 2: Type Control with "T" to format the fonT.

Step 3: Skip suggested rectangular palette colors; **choose "more colors."**

Is there an objective, simple way to decide if a color is light, dark, or medium?

Yes, and it's easy. The secret follows.

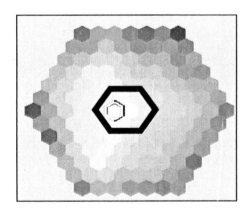

Step 4: The hexagon palette appears whenever "more colors..." is selected.

Pick either a very dark color (outside 2 rings) font color, or a very light (1 inside ring) font color. **Make the background (fill color) the opposite of the font color in bright/dark extremes,**

This ensures high color contrast and good legibility. It eliminates rings 2, 3, 4 and 5 counting from the center.

Pick 1 very dark font and 1 very light (or white) background shade for maximum contrast or else pick the exact opposite- a bright white font on a very dark background.

Change font color in Powerpoint© 2007

The Font Color button on the Font Tab

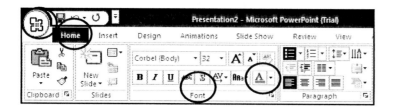

On the "Home" menu choice of the Ribbon in Powerpoint© 2007 look for the "Font" tab. It is 3rd from the left in the screen print. Tool bar buttons with a colored bar beneath the letter "A" display a color palette.

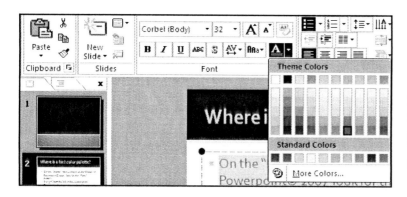

The 2007 font color palette is organized from very light to very dark.

Change the font color in new slide shows to very dark or else to extremely light (white) depending on your background. Text must be the opposite of the background's brightness.

Change Background Color in Ppt© 2007

There was no Control Key shortcut for this in PPT 2003 so the next fastest approach is to right-click an object. To change all the slides make the change to the Slide Master by choosing View, Slide Master on the Ribbon menu.

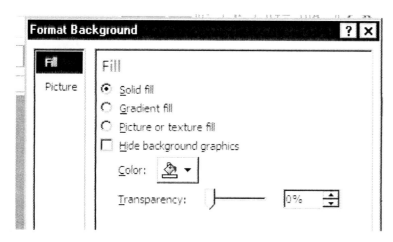

To change only one slide right-click that slide and choose the last option, Format Background.

Select either Fill or Picture on the left pane. We will pick Fill.

For simplicity choose Solid Fill. Choose the lightest possible background color to contrast with black font.

There are several other ways to figure out where to click to get the work done. We leave open at all times the cross reference help file in Excel entitled "Where PPT 2003 commands are in 2007.xlsx" If we had used that method we would see the following.

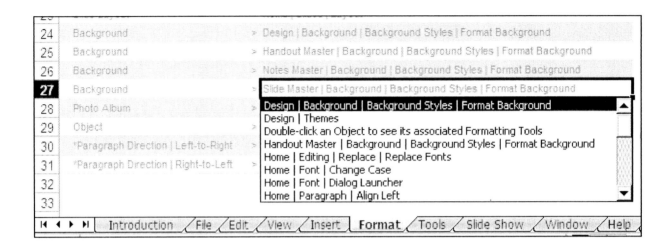

We would consult the tab heading FORMAT then in column A look beside A27 which says BACKGROUND. We would actually right-click the cell B27 and choose to see the associated DROP DOWN LIST. The Screen Print above shows it opened. The first five of nine list box choices appear to be relevant to our task which we already finished.

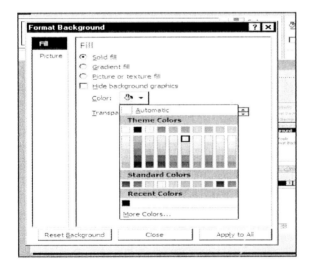

If we delve further here are the color choices for FORMAT BACKGROUND (left).

Obviously for high contrast if we already want black text we just pick one the light shades at the top row. For example, the top rectangle in the column for red is an attractive shade of pink. The color choices in 2007 are much improved.

Wasted Space In Text Placeholders

As we look (below) at slides we created in View, Slide Show mode, we notice they do not seem "balanced." All the text is bunched at the top near the title. All the extra space is below the last line of text. White space below the last text is known as **wasted space**. A bulleted list box without many words leaves so much empty space inside its boundary that it creates editing problems. Leaving it oversized may interfere with selecting smaller objects like images or photos.

Wasted space can be evened out from top to bottom and trimmed off the right side. Extra placeholder space can be adjusted so the slide has room to place a graphic. Nearly all slides need a graphic image relevant to the topic. Sometimes the font needs to be enlarged.

Even out the white space

Select the text place holder checkered (all). Click once inside it and hit the Escape key in the upper left of the keyboard. Position it using the ARROW navigation keys on the lower right keyboard area. Click keyboard arrow keys to move a tiny distance, hold the "gas pedal" down to go fast!

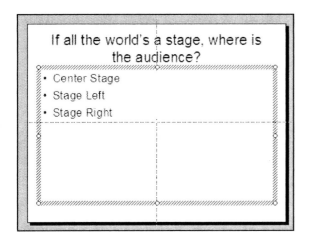

This figure shows a textbox with white circles called resizing handles. It has a slanted line border.

Hitting the ESCAPE key makes the selection checkered, or selected ALL for moving.

ARROW keys move the checkered object efficiently

Dragging resizing handles reshapes it.

Drag the appropriate resizing handle (white circles on the border) to reshape the text placeholder. Drag the one in the bottom, center, towards the third bullet (up). Drag the right edge's center circle toward the left. Leaving the excess wasted space in placeholders causes difficulty selecting smaller objects on a slide. Before we resize text boxes and move them around, we want to place relevant images on our slides so we only reshape placeholders once per slide.

Learning From Cognitive Psychology

Three brain regions exist. They handle 1) perception and sensory stores; 2) short-term or working memory; 3) long-term memory [2]

Selective Perception and the Sensory Stores

We receive more events stimulating our senses than we can concentrate on. We translate only part of what we pay attention to, for later storage in memory. We notice what we expect to see from experience. We find things interesting when they are related to what we already know, or if they are so new they force us to attend to them.

Designing for Selective Perception

Showing a picture on every slide helps the audience form a bridge to the slide content since they are already trying to picture what it means to them. Displaying slide titles that describe the contents at the next higher category level aids the brain in encoding data for storage. If a bullet item appears after a photo it will attract attention. It is distracting to have exploding, flying or bouncing text animations.

Limits on Short Term Memory

Sensory memories store complete records of what we pay attention to, but they last only very briefly before they decay and vanish. Before the data decays, we make note of the links or relationships among the statements in the new record and also encode it into a more permanent memory; or else we lose the record.

Presenters can boost the effectiveness of their presentations by organizing information into a compare / contrast format. Spend time to show relationships among the facts presented. Explicitly link new knowledge to existing knowledge.

---

[2] Retrieved May 11 from www.foshay.org/PDFs/COGNITIVEAPPROACH.pdf. Extracted from *Foshay, W.R., Silber, K.H., & Stelnicki, M.B. (2003). Writing Training Materials That Work: How to Train Anyone to Do Anything. San Francisco: Pfeiffer.*

Rip Out Test 6

Cognitive Psychology

Sensory Store Memory

Print Your Name (& class time or section number.)
Score _ _ out of ___total

Print the letter of the best answers to these questions in the **left margin**.

1. Which of these is NOT a distinct area in our brains?
   a) Sensory stores; b) Short term memory
   c) Long term memory d) Latent storage
2. Which of these do we translate into long term memory?
   a. Anything we pay attention to
   b. Things related to what we already know from experience
   c. Things related to survival
   d. The loudest stimulus (like TV ads) in the environment
3. (True/False) The more large photos, and the fewer words, as on a Title Only Autolayout, the more effective the presentation is.
5. Placing a relevant photo on every slide
   a. Forms a cognitive bridge b. Provides visual variety
   c. Is not always possible d. Is called chunking
6. Why embed questions among our content slides?
   a. The end of the show is too late b. To stimulate links
   c. For active not passive rehearsal d. For all the above
7. Presenters should strive to show more linkable examples with
   a. Bulleted text b. Photographs
   c. Video clips d. Compare / contrast tables

Rehearsal means creating associations

When we mentally rehearse information it is passed from the short-lived sensory stores to longer term memory. Rehearsal does not mean passively repeating the information. Rehearsal is done by creating associations.

Designing for Bulleted Text

It is distracting, irritating and eventually boring to have text fly around the screen. Audiences at first try to read moving text, find they cannot do so, and attend to outside street traffic instead of the complexity of those immature animation effects. It is sufficient to let text appear as revealed in some animated geometric pattern. The only animation effect perceived as more boring than text that moves around, is text that moves around slowly. Custom Animation speeds must be chosen from only **very fast or fast;** not even medium.

A slide show should grab and focus attention on the desired objectives. Custom animation is a tool for doing that. The best attention-grabbing tool ever invented is for the presenter to interact with the audience. If a presenter builds up both motivation and confidence throughout the slide show the audience will remain engaged.

Limited capacity-

Research repeatedly shows short term memory is limited in both quantity and duration. We can remember 7 +/- 2 bits of information at most. To remember more we have to "chunk" (or group) bits of information such as calling the first three digits of a phone number an area code though that term has lost any meaning.

Observation of many a slide show audience shows the maximum number of bullet points an audience will tolerate is four maximum per slide. At that point short term or sensory stores are fully occupied and hearing the fifth point is possible only while dumping the first point. It is hard to admit adding a fifth bullet to a slide is a waste of everybody's time.

Rip Out Test 7

Cognitive Psychology

Capacity

Print Your Name (& class time or section number.)
Score __ _ out of ___total

Print the letter of the best answers to these questions in the **left margin.**

1. Text that flies around the monitor
   a) Grabs needed attention
   b) Relieves boredom
   c) Distracts and bores
   d) Speeds comprehension
2. The best attention grabber, the most valuable, is _?
   a. Sounds
   b. Custom Animation
   c. Interaction with a live Presenter
   d. Multimedia
3. (True/False) Calling part of a phone number the Area Code allows us to stretch short term memory to 10 digits instead of 7.
4. Custom animation calls positive attention to text when it is
   a. Fast   b. Medium   c. Slow   d. Flying
5. Audiences tolerate at MOST, how many bullets on one slide?
   a. 2   b. 4   c. 6   d. 8
6. Which of these animation effects is best for bulleted text?
   a. Fly in   b. Crawl in   c. Dissolve in   d. Bounce in
7. How many bits of information can we remember hearing, at most?
   a. 3   b. 4-6   c. 5-9   d. 6 +/- 3
8. A live Presenter, interacting with the audience, can _?
   a. Build motivation
   b. Build confidence
   b. Rehearse and review
   d. All the above

Designing for Limited Capacity - Chunking

1) Breaking a large body of knowledge into smaller, easy to digest segments is called "**chunking**" the material. Even a hungry wolf tears off only what it is able to drag off and defend. If we don't chunk our slide presentations the audience will chunk it for themselves by doing an immediate memory dump.
2) Designing for the limited capacity and duration of short term sensory input requires analogies to link new information to existing knowledge. The wolf example above is an analogy of chunking.
3) Slide show presentation software allows us to present the information in multiple formats such as verbal, graphic, auditory and visual. We can link to the web and show video clip examples.
4) Boost the movement from rehearsal to encoding in long-term memory. Embedding question slides throughout the slide show ensures some audience members will rearrange the material just heard so they can construct a verbal answer.

The information being rehearsed is not yet organized and encoded (formatted) the way it will be when it is finally stored in memory. There are separate spaces in the brain for storing and rehearsing verbal information and for visual/spatial information.

Long Term Memory

- The strength of a memory increases each time we practice rehearsing (associations) and recalling the memory. Two practice sessions are four times as strong as one; while three sessions are nine times stronger than one.
- Adding more information to what we need to learn strengthens memory. As we tie the new information to existing knowledge, we create more routes to return to it.
- Memories are stored in "chunks," of about seven pieces.
- We use a linear code for verbal information and a spatial code for visual information. We encode text in different areas than we do graphics.
- Building the information into a hierarchy adds more sorting

handles for recalling the information. Concept maps and images help in several ways.

Implications for designers-

1) To build in meaningful practice, embed questions, exercises and problems throughout the slide show.

2) Provide hyperlinks with elaborating information.

3) Break the information in meaningful "chunks" of appropriate size.

4) Show the information so it links both verbal and visual information

5) Organize the information hierarchically by studying Concept Maps or collaborating on such a Map with learners.

6) Cross-link many associations to the information.

7) Embed authentic (real-world) contexts for explanations, examples, and practice problems.

On the Master Slide

In MS PPT© 2003 and O.O.©Impress

Changes to a Master slide apply globally to all slides; yet global changes may be overruled locally on individual slides.

The Master slide has a default (automatic) format of Sentence case where only the first word has a capital letter. Other choices toggling with **Shift + F3** are all lowercase and all uppercase. Shift + F3 does not show Title case, which capitalizes every major word but not articles (a, an, or the) nor short prepositions (for, in, to, of). To specify Title case as the default:

Click the menu choices View, Master, Slide Master. Select the title placeholder as checkered-border, as if for moving. Click the menu choices **Format, Change Case...**, **Title Case, OK**. To return to editing mode, click on View, Normal. Only do this once for the whole show. Every slide's title placeholder will have Title case.

Many will choose all capitals; but this is an error in judgment. We have never read a book written in all capitals. It slows comprehension.

Set the Title Placeholder Case

in MS PowerPoint© 2007

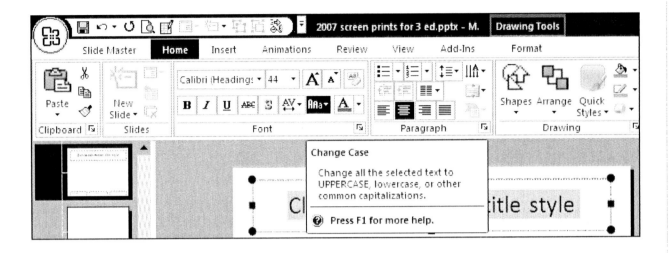

Click on View, on the Quick Access Menu Bar, then click the Slide Master button on the Ribbon. Once on the Slide Master place the cursor anywhere in the Title Placeholder then hit the Escape Key on the keyboard to select it ALL (solid border line). Next click the Home menu choice on the Quick Access Menu Bar then hunt through the tool bar buttons on the third Ribbon tab heading, Font.

Find the Case toolbar button and click it.

The nearest fit to Title Case is "Capitalize every word." Title case if available, would not capitalize prepositions less than five letters long.

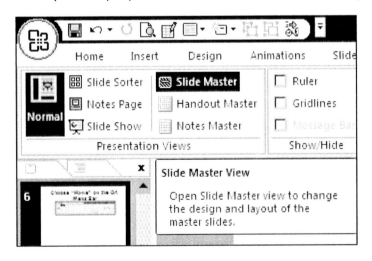

The Master Slide controls or forms a backdrop or background for all slides. To see it we click on VIEW, then SLIDE MASTER.

Select the Master Slide's Title Placeholder ALL or with a solid border.

Hold the SHIFT KEY down while we click inside the Title textbox place holder.

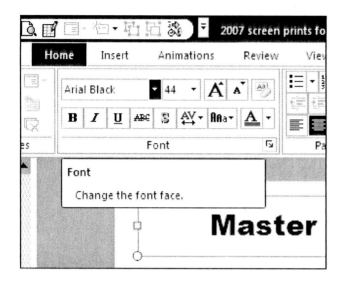

Click the Quack (Quick Access) menu choices **HOME, then FONT** or else use Control + T. On the dialog box for formatting font,

CHANGE the name of the font by typing "Arial Black" where it says "Calibri".

Calibri is a good body text but is too thin to make a title that stands out. **Arial Black** is more legible and puts more ink down.

Hit the ESCAPE KEY in the uppermost left corner of the keyboard. That de-selects the Title Placeholder. Shift + Click on the Master Slide's Bulleted Textbox. Or click inside the bulleted list box then hit the ESCAPE KEY. The goal is to select it ALL with a solid border line.

Click the Ribbon menu choices HOME, then FONT or else use Control + T. On the dialog box for formatting font, CHANGE the name of the font by typing "Comic Sans MS" where it currently says "Calibri". Hit OK then look through your slides. The list will scroll to match what you type. When you type the first three letters ("Com…") of the font face name you will be able to see Comic Sans MS and click to choose it.

Arial Black puts more ink on a slide than other fonts so it is good for titles. But never add BOLD formatting to Arial Black. **Arial Black has wide, generous kerning (space between letters).** Look closely. Every letter has white space on both sides of the letter. This is the number one characteristic to look for when deciding on a font.

Comic Sans MS has the same wide kerning. Because it looks hand printed some businesses do not allow it. If so, substitute VERDANA font for it. Verdana font face has 30% wider spaces between letters than Arial does. Calibri is a good body text. Return to editing by clicking the menu choices **VIEW then NORMAL**.

A Highly Readable Font

The left slide shows 8 font faces, ranked by the author. These are candidates for bulleted text. We already chose Arial Black for the Title Placeholder.

8 Fonts - Most Legible on Top

- Wide Kerning (Consolas)
- Wide Kerning (Papyrus)
- Wide Kerning (Helvetica)
- Wide Kerning (MS Sans Serif)
- Wide Kerning (Candara)
- Wide Kerning (Stylus BT)
- Wide Kerning (Calibri)
- Wide Kerning (Kidprint)

Ensure a font face for bullets is very legible by selecting Comic Sans MS, Papyrus, Stylus BT, or Kidprint for your coursework or an **informal** slide show.

For a **formal** business talk choose instead from Verdana, Consolas, Helvetica, MS Sans Serif, Candara, or the default font named Calibri.

Animate a Master Slide Bullet Box

The bulleted list box for the Slide Master does not need a case specified. We changed the default fonts to nicer, more legible font faces immediately above. If we lend animation to the bulleted list box on the master slide we animate every slide.

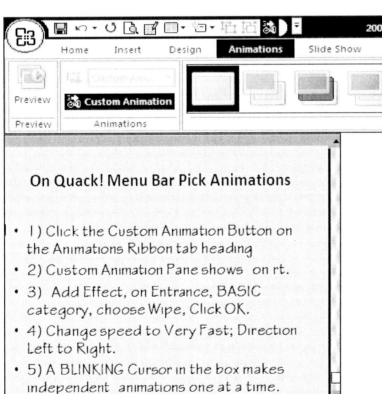

On Quack! Menu Bar Pick Animations

- 1) Click the Custom Animation Button on the Animations Ribbon tab heading
- 2) Custom Animation Pane shows on rt.
- 3) Add Effect, on Entrance, BASIC category, choose Wipe, Click OK.
- 4) Change speed to Very Fast; Direction Left to Right.
- 5) A BLINKING Cursor in the box makes independent animations one at a time.

See Screen Print on left. On the Quack Menu Bar click ANIMATIONS, then Custom Animation Button.

Animation of text should never move it around on the screen. What's left? We can pick from 16 of the 19 effects listed as "Basic." Most have names like basic shapes such as box, circle, diamond, ellipse and so on.

Three other good animations include blinds, dissolve, or **wipe**. We would choose Wipe. Since the default direction is wipe from bottom to top, not good, we change the details to **wipe from left to right**.

Final choice is what speed. Watching the audience reaction during 3,500 student presentations the author believes the audience would tell you: there are 3 speeds available: **Very Fast, Fast and Lost Your Audience.**

Both flying text and slow speeds are boring to an audience. A Very Fast Wipe animation will look like an invisible printer is printing it out as you present.

Bullets need to appear one whole bullet item at a time not one word at a time. To ensure independent behavior select the bullet placeholder for editing – the cursor will be **blinking**. Nothing will show selection. If as much as an empty space is selected the bullets will all arrive at once.

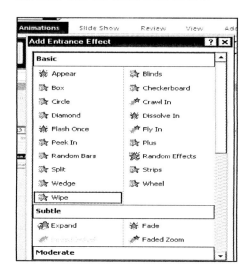

After clicking the Animations, Custom Animation Button we click on the Add Effect Button, choose On Entrance, and come down the list below the horizontal spacer to choose "More Effects…"

Wipe is at the bottom left of the **Basic** category.

Assignment 1: Text Placeholders

Objectives: Use keyboard shortcuts in the Outline Tab heading to enter titles and bulleted text on slides; move, resize and reshape text placeholders to eliminate dead space; recognize placeholder patterns and change border look of text placeholders; format the Master Slide; use the views Normal, Slide Sorter and Slide Show; use the Outline Tab and the Slides tab heading in the left window.

Start Power Point to a BLANK NEW PRESENTATION. Maximize it.

Do **NOT** start with a MS Design Template.

We will abbreviate PowerPoint© as PPT

On the menu bar click FILE, SAVE AS.

Change the top drop down list box to your **class work** folder.

Name the presentation Profound Questions- Your Last Name on slide one. **SAVE AS "PQ-1.ppt"**

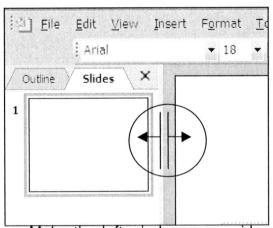

This requires finding the sweet spot first.

Slowly move the mouse from left to right across the PPT window. The left window has a vertical scroll bar.

When you reach the far edge of this scroll bar **your mouse changes from a pointer arrow to a 2-headed arrow** which signifies dragging will resize the selected object

Make the left window pane wider. Drag the right edge of the left window toward the right.

.See above figure.
1) DRAG toward the right with the left mouse button down.
2) When it can't drag any wider, halt. (As if you had a choice here)
3) Look at the left window. There are two TAB HEADINGS.
4) The tab on top by default is SLIDES tab. It shows thumbnail size graphics.
5) One tab heading says OUTLINE. Click to select OUTLINE TAB.
6) Now drag the left window even wider than before. Why is this?
7) Microsoft originally designed the same keyboard controls for making a numbered outline in MS WORD identical to the OUTLINE TAB heading in PPT.
8) Knowing we need more space horizontally, MS made the allowable width of OUTLINE tab much larger than for SLIDES tab.
9) It's a good thing it makes the middle, main editing window, too small to read for now. We are about to make that area untidy.
10) Put the mouse pointer on the right of slide one's icon in OUTLINE tab.
11) It should be a blinking cursor.
12) TYPE Profound Questions
13) Hit the Enter Key.
14) Hit the Tab Key once.
15) TYPE Your name and class time (Hernandez, noon)
16) Hit the Enter Key.
17) Hold the SHIFT Key down with the right hand and strike the Tab Key one time.

NOTICE how on a new line, Tab Key indents to the right, while SHIFT with TAB goes backward, to the left, or promotes the outline level. Notice that we must hit the Enter key **before** we switch from bullets to Slide Titles and back. This point will be practiced in the exercise multiple times. If this did not happen, repeat direction step 4 d. OUTLINE tab heading is in the left window pane of normal view.

18) Place the cursor blinking to the right of a newly numbered slide 2 in OUTLINE tab.
19) Type the Title of slide 2 as "If all the world is a stage where's the audience?" without quotation marks.

20) Hit the Enter Key for a new line. We get a new slide but want a series of bullets instead.
21) Hit the TAB key to make the new line bulleted.
22) TYPE "Stage Left"
23) ENTER
24) TYPE "Stage Right"
25) ENTER
26) TYPE "Back Stage"
27) Hit the ENTER key then
28) HOLD the SHIFT key down while you strike TAB key one time.

The Outline Tab in the left window will look like this.

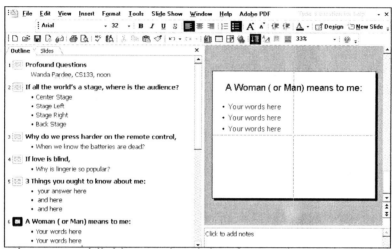

29) Place the cursor blinking to the right of a newly numbered slide 3. OUTLINE tab
30) Type the Title of slide 3 as "Why do we press harder on the remote control" without the quotation marks.
31) ENTER
32) TAB
33) TYPE "When we know the batteries are dead"?
34) Hit the ENTER key then
35) HOLD the SHIFT key down while striking TAB one time.
36) See that the cursor blink to the right of a newly numbered slide 4. OUTLINE tab
37) Type the Title of slide 4 as "If love is blind," without quotation marks.
38) ENTER
39) TAB
40) TYPE "Why is lingerie so popular"?
41) Hit the ENTER key then
42) HOLD the SHIFT key down while you strike TAB key one time.
43) See the cursor blinking to the right of a newly numbered slide 5.OUTLINE tab
44) Type the Title of slide 5 as "Three things people should know about me:" without quotation marks.
45) ENTER
46) TAB
47) TYPE in your own words for point 1.
48) ENTER
49) TYPE in your own words for points 2 and 3. Use ENTER between bullets

50) Hit the ENTER key then
51) HOLD the SHIFT key down as we strike the TAB key one time.
52) The cursor is blinking to the right of a newly numbered slide 6. OUTLINE tab
53) If you are a woman, Type the Title of slide 6 as "A Man Means to Me" without quotation marks.
54) If you are a man, Type the Title of slide 6 as "A Woman Means to Me" without quotation marks.
55) If the above directions are not clear, ask an older student what "Opposite Gender" means. Changes in the FCC Decency Act prohibit us from clarifying this point.
56) ENTER
57) TAB
58) TYPE "your first point" in your own words as you see fit.
59) Create two other bullets.

Different VIEWS for different tasks.

Click the tab heading in the left side which is labeled "SLIDES." Notice how it shows a miniature thumbnail of whole slides but not outline structure. If we had already placed graphics on slides the graphics would show on the SLIDES heading but not in OUTLINE tab.

Make the left window narrow again to see the middle area better.

SLIDE SORTER

CLICK the menu choices VIEW, then SLIDE SORTER. Here are operations you can do in SLIDE SORTER VIEW:

1) Right click any slide then choose Control X to CUT it.
2) Click between any two slides. A vertical blinking line appears. Right click and choose PASTE. We could have drug the slide around instead.
3) Drag any slide except the title slide to a new position.
4) IF (but we don't now) want to delete a slide we click once to select it then hit the DELETE key on the keyboard upper right.
5) IF we wanted a new slide after the cursor we would use the combination Control + M for MORE SLIDES. Try this now.
6) To reverse the last action above use Control + Z for UNDO last command. Try this now.
7) IF we wanted to edit a slide we would DOUBLE CLICK it in Slide Sorter View. Try this now.

Click the menu choices VIEW, SLIDE SHOW. During the show use these 12 commands.

1) First find the PAGE DOWN key on your upper right of the keyboard. Use it to go through the show forward.
2) Use the PAGE UP key to go backward in a show.
3) Use the space bar to advance forward.
4) Use the Enter Key to advance forward.
5) Use the letter P to return to the PREVIOUS slide.
6) Use the UP ARROW key at the lower right of the key board to visit the previous slide.
7) Use the letter N key to advance to the NEXT slide.
8) Use the DOWN ARROW key to advance forward through the show.

9) IF YOU bump out of SLIDE SHOW VIEW back to editing go to any slide and hold down SHIFT while you hit the FUNCTION 5 key at the top of the keyboard, F5.

10) While in SLIDE SHOW view, type a number from 1 to 6 and you go to that slide. This is handy.

11) Strike the letter "a" to see the pointer as an ARROW.

12) Control + P changes the pointer into a PEN. Scribble with it. Underline some phrase. Circle a bulleted item.

This ends part 1 of PQ-1 directions. Typing in OUTLINE tab heading, we have put the words into text placeholders without actually typing in a text placeholder. **This is the key to saving 75% of the time** it would take most people to create the text for a new slide show.

As we tour our recently created PPT show it we notice the slides do not seem "balanced." All the text is bunched at the top near the title. All the extra space is below the last line of text. White space below the last text is known as wasted space.

Wasted space can be evened out top to bottom so there is the same empty space above the title as below the title. Space can be adjusted so there is room to place a graphic. Nearly all slides could use a graphic image that is relevant to the topic. Sometimes the font needs to be enlarged. Reshaping textboxes is frequently needed.

Two ways to even out or proportion the white space on a slide:

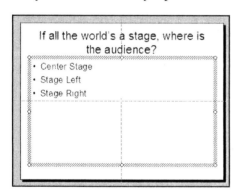

This figure shows a textbox with white circles called resizing handles.

It has slanted lines for an editing border. Hitting the ESCAPE key makes the selection checkered, or selected ALL for moving.

The goal is to even out all the unused space so there is neat, evenly balanced look to the slide. The slide shown can be made more manageable if we decrease the width and height of the text box.

Drag the appropriate **resizing handle** (white circles on the border) to resize or reshape the text placeholder. The white circles around the border are designed to reshape text boxes when dragged.

- Drag the one in the **bottom center**, upwards the third bullet.
- Drag the **right edge's center circle** toward the left.

Leaving the excess wasted space in them causes difficulty selecting smaller objects on a slide.

Locate RELEVANT images

Before we resize text boxes and move them around, we want to **place relevant images** on our slides so we only do it once per slide. Relevant images help make your bullet points easier to remember.

We use the Web browser named **Mozilla Firefox.** At the time these directions were written, Mozilla did not have as many security flaws to fear as Internet Explorer. So that the right click menus match the directions please use Mozilla Firefox.

Go to Mozilla.org on the Web. Download Firefox. It is FREE, open source programming. While on their web site, download their free email program, called **Mozilla Thunderbird.** Open Mozilla Firefox the web browser.

Use the Web browser to go to the **Google.com** web site and click on **IMAGES** directly above the search window. (Don't use the tiny desktop search bar; go to Google.com – there is a huge difference in the search results.)

In Google Image Search, type either "profound" or "think" or "question" or something related to the theme of answering tough questions for the title slide. Have PPT open. The hit list returns photographs about the search phrase. When you find a nice image that fits your topic **right click it** and choose **Copy.**

Switch to the open PPT show by using the task bar buttons along the bottom of the monitor screen. Right click slide one, and choose **paste. Select** the recently pasted picture. It should show resizing handles along its edges. **Use the ARROW Keys** at the keyboard's lower right to move it into a good place. DRAG one of its four CORNER resizing handles to resize the picture.

An example - the graphic question marks was Pasted; Moved; wasted space was removed from text boxes; Placeholders were resized and reshaped using corner handles.

All elements were evenly spaced top to bottom.

Go to slide 2, all the world is a stage.

Think of an appropriate search phrase and type it in Mozilla Firefox, (Or IE or Netscape) into Google (Image Search). Try audience, stage, theater, theatre . Just as in step 3 and step 4, find a relevant picture, Copy it, Switch back to PPT using the bottom task bar buttons. Right click slide 2 and paste it.

Continue until each slide has one graphic on it. Even out the white space above and below titles, left and right of photos, etc. so it looks organized and symmetrical not lopsided.

In Blackboard, or WebCT, or however the instructor decides, **SUBMIT this file** calling it "PQ-1 Text" in the COURSE DOCUMENTS (or alternate) folder. Check with your professor or instructor to see if they want it submitted differently.

Five principles for choice of font:

1) Kerning – look for white space between every letter of every word. (True Type or Mono spaced fonts)
2) Size – smallest font size on a slide is at least 28 pts. Above 28 is better.
3) Sans Serif – no fancy, frilly headers and footers on the letters. This eliminates Times New Roman. Sorry.
4) Use highly contrasting colors in text boxes – one very light, the other very dark.
5) Avoid special effects such as shadow, underline, italic, bold; use color instead.

Wide Kerning (True Type)

This first slide shows three fonts that do not have wide kerning. The second slide will show three fonts with excellent kerning.

Wide Kerning = resolution

All these are 32 points. The text stretching furthest for the same words has best kerning (unless it is a serif font).

1. Wide kerning (space between letters)?

   Times New Roman –poor (a serif font)
2. Wide kerning (space between letters)?

   Arial - mediocre
3. Wide kerning (space between letters)?

   Haettenschweiler

The next PPT slide below shows 3 examples of excellent kerning. When you choose a font face, study how much separation space (white space) is on both sides of every letter. This choice impacts every slide in your show.

47

```
┌─────────────────────────────────────────────┐
│                                               │
│        **Wide Kerning Examples**              │
│                                               │
│        All font samples are 32 points size.   │
│                                               │
│   **1. Wide kerning (space between**          │
│      **letters)**                             │
│        **– Arial Black = excellent for titles** │
│   2. Wide kerning (space between              │
│      letters)                                 │
│        – Verdana = excellent for bulleted text│
│   3. Wide kerning (space between letters)     │
│        – Comic Sans MS = excellent for text   │
│                                               │
└─────────────────────────────────────────────┘
```

When choosing a font face, look first for wide separation spacing (kerning). **Verdana** is better than Times New Roman and Arial. **Comic Sans MS** is more readable than Verdana, but is too informal (looks hand printed) to suit some business people. **Arial Black** is great for title placeholders.

The next slide shows eight easy-to-read fonts for text placeholders.

```
┌─────────────────────────────────────────────┐
│                                               │
│       8 Fonts - Most Legible on Top           │
│                                               │
│   • Wide Kerning (Consolas)                   │
│   • Wide Kerning (Papyrus)                    │
│   • Wide Kerning (Helvetica)                  │
│   • Wide Kerning (MS Sans Serif)              │
│   • Wide Kerning (Candara)                    │
│   • Wide Kerning (Stylus BT)                  │
│   • Wide Kerning (Calibri)                    │
│   • Wide Kerning (Kidprint)                   │
│                                               │
└─────────────────────────────────────────────┘
```

Size 28 Points

Pick a sans serif font with wide kerning (True Type). All body text should be at least 28 points size. Title text should be even larger. Let's consider legibility from the projector and legibility of the printouts (Handouts).

Projector: If the font is sans serif, has wide kerning, and high color contrast, then the audience can read 28 point font at the back of a huge room (50-60 feet away). The author teaches in a huge lab. The distance to the back corners is so large, a remote wireless microphone and public address speaker are required just for students to hear the instructor. But students easily read 28 point text.

Printouts: To save paper, toner, and best of all save time, printouts are usually made as "Handouts," 6 slides per page. Change the "Print What" drop down list box from "Slides" to "Handouts" shown below as tip #1.

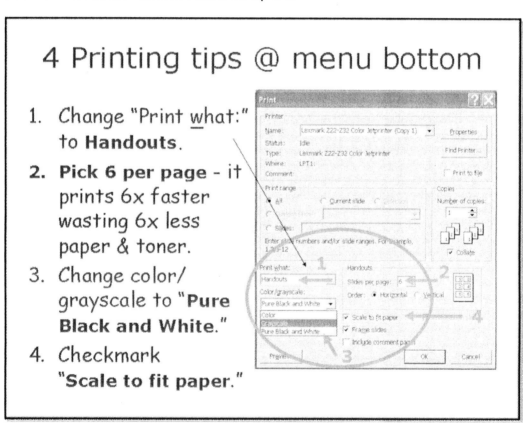

4 Printing tips @ menu bottom

1. Change "Print what:" to **Handouts**.

2. **Pick 6 per page** - it prints 6x faster wasting 6x less paper & toner.

3. Change color/ grayscale to "**Pure Black and White.**"

4. Checkmark "**Scale to fit paper.**"

Benefits of Big Fonts

Bigger font is better – even if it makes you double the number of slides you intended to use. There are many reasons beside legibility. Cognitive psychologists like uncrowded, uncluttered slides because uncluttered slides reduce the possibility of **cognitive overload** – too much, too fast.

Placing 28 point font in the bulleted list box makes a limit of four maximum bullets on any slide seem easy to follow.

Pause between slides

If you remember to pause instead of race to the next slide, it is easier to remember your points. Rest the audience's ears and it helps the audience remember better what they last heard. When you click to have the next bulleted item appear, give the audience a minute to read it, then talk.

Recall

Every person has a sensory store limit of 7 plus or minus 2 facts or pieces of data they can hold at one time. Then they have to dump one of those existing 5 – 9 to deal with the next piece of new data. Usually people do this by forgetting something they just heard, to accommodate new. Giving them a pacing break lets them retain what is in sensory store by moving previous input to the short term memory store. Asking the audience frequent questions which make them rearrange the material helps them remember the points long term.

REM

During REM sleep at night, information is moved from short term memory and recorded in long term memory. If a person gets no REM sleep, or even worse, no sleep at all, that day's learning is lost. If we present as fast as we can talk, the information is lost during the first step, the sensory input stage. Pausing on slides and between slides boosts effectiveness by helping those who reflect on the material, to transfer it from sensory store to short term memory. Large font size aids this by limiting what will fit on a slide.

brevity

Big letters force *brevity*. Fewer words are better. Forced to shorten our sentences, we use active voice (subject – verb- object) not passive. It's yet another gain for the audience. Audiences read and understand active voice better than passive voice.

We will get rid of ~~all of the~~ prepositional phrases, then it reads better. Using 28 point font boost retention. To say more effective words on a slide, stick with large font size. Learn to say what is essential using fewer words. It will come across as crisp, snappy, and well prepared. It will be more pleasant to experience.

Pure Black & White

What does changing the choice "Color / Grayscale" to "Pure Black & White" do for you?

It leaves photographs and clip art as grayscale. But if you used color inside textboxes it bleaches that to black on white with no shades of gray, for printing enhancement only. Otherwise a non-color printer will produce gray on gray, which will make handouts nearly unreadable.

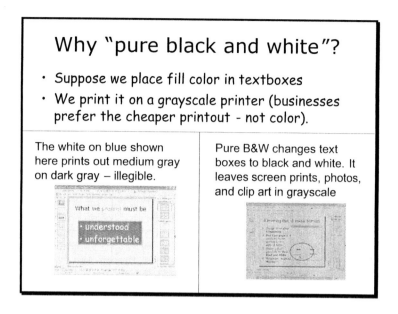

Plain, Sans Serif Fonts

... are easy to read. The term comes from French. Sans Serif is pronounced "Sa Seree," as though the letters "n" and "s" in Sans were not there. Sans means "without." The second word, Serif, is pronounced like it was spelled "Seree" not "Serif." Sans Serif describes a font face having no fancy, frilly headers and footers on the tops and bottoms of straight stroke letters. Of course, this eliminates Times New Roman font face, but MS was not qualified to choose fonts for us in the first place.

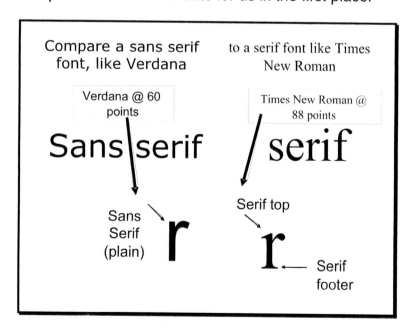

Inspect the slide above. Reading off a monitor or projector screen is not the same as reading a book or newspaper. It has been claimed that serif font faces were superior because the little curly tops and bottoms "guide the reader's eye to the next letter." This claim is dubious if not humorous. It is doubtful that sans serif font face interferes with the process of reading left to right. What using a serif font obviously does, that is bad, is encroach on the white space between letters, decreasing the kerning necessary for resolution.

Key to Color- Extreme Contrast

Either the text must be very dark or the fill color (slide background color) very light, or the opposite must be true. No medium shades belong inside textboxes. The human eye recognizes language when the words or symbols contrast sufficiently to the background. Here, all that matters is the difference in shades of darkness not whether the color is fashionable. We are looking for two extremes: light and dark regardless of absolute color.

There are always two colors to choose, text and the color behind the text. In turn, the color behind text is either slide background color or textbox fill color.

Legibility & Font Color

Ninety percent of our message, our meaning, is carried by text; words we say or play back, and words we display. Any audience will bring 2 requirements. Words we say or play must be audible and make sense; words we display must be both legible and easy to understand.

Few people are mindful of legibility but no audience will strain to read your words. Most people like or dislike a font for obscure reasons related to fashion, or equally mythical, artistic quality. Having watched thousands of term project presentations, it is obvious the number one factor your audience needs is legibility; cute is way down the list of design factors. Being unable to read the text causes boredom.

Compounding the problem, no current PPT book takes the time and space to illustrate what factors make a font legible. We at least try in this section.

Most students think when they are choosing text color, they are obviously choosing color; however, they are ought to choose the contrast between light and dark, not the color shade itself.

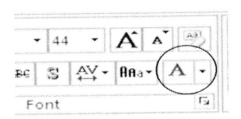

The choice of color shades (light versus dark) is easier in PPPT© 2007.

To change **font color** click the Home menu choice. See the left figure.

The second ribbon tab heading is Font (under the buttons).

The circled button is Font Color.

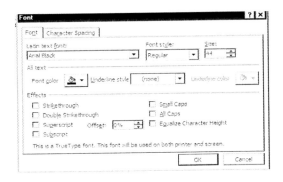

Select some text, use **Control + T to show the Format, Font** dialog box, and change the color. Also add or remove Font Special Effects here.

The left figure shows a format font dialog box in PPT© 2007.

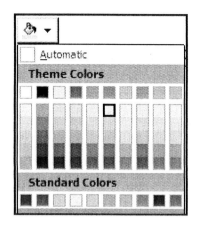

Open the drop down list box for the circled font color button to see an **objective definition of light and dark**. Powerpoint© 2003 provides "More colors" which presents a hexagon color palette which solves that problem.

In Powerpoint© 2007 initial color choices are presented organized top to bottom from lightest to darkest. This is a huge improvement. See the left figure.

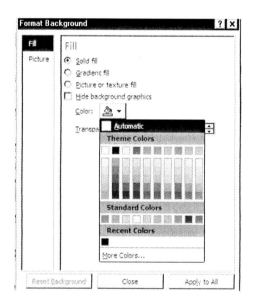

To get the same color choice dialog for a slide background we would select a slide background instead of text.

Right click a slide, away from text boxes, and choose the last line, Format Background...

The dialog box to the left appears. Click the arrow head beside the Color Button and pick from the palette already organized by lightest to darkest shade in 20% increments.

Special effects Control + T

can be added to text from the Format, Font menu. A rapid way to open the format font dialog box is use Control + T. (Control + F had been reserved for opening the **find utility,** so MS gave the shortcut to the last letter of the word "font.")
- Special effects can be added to a few key words to emphasize them.
- Most special effects are overused and make the text harder to read.
- In MS Word© boldface best grabs attention without obscuring the text.
- In MS Powerpoint© making text a different color is the best special effect.

Six special effects

in order of a) attention-grabbing & b) readability are:

1) Change the color of words to grab attention. But not yellow on white.
2) Bold face calls attention to a large font size and it is usually still legible. For small font, boldface still grabs attention but is often not legible. Avoid the temptation to bold face too much. Bold face is not used with Arial Black. Adding bold to Arial Black smudges words with letters such as "e" and "a."

53

3) Italic font is less noticeable and demands less attention but is usually legible if kept to a few words.
4) Underlining isn't this paragraph hard to read? We need white space both below & between letters. Changing the color of font beats underlining.
5) ALL CAPS IS HARDER TO READ. EVER READ A BOOK IN ALL CAPS?
6) Shadow font is inherently fuzzy. Why would the presenter even focus the projector? It was supposed to give the text an artistic 3-D effect but it frequently looks unfocused. Nearly every design template applies the shadow effect to text. Trying to read it gives some of us headaches.

Five Text Design Decisions - Review

Use only very dark or very light colors in a text box, but never medium.

Choose a font face with wide kerning (white space between letters)

Choose a sans serif font face, one without frilly bars.

Use 28 points or larger font size for body text.

The best special effect is a different color.

(The worst special effects are shadow, underline, all caps, italic and for a few font faces, bold.)

Bold face calls attention to a large font size and it is legible. For small font, boldface best calls out for attention but is not as legible.

ALL CAPS IS HARDER TO READ. EVER READ A BOOK IN ALL CAPS?

Shadow font is fuzzy. Why even focus the projector?

Open Book Test 1

First try to answer what is easily recalled. Look up the answers in the previous pages. **Immediate feedback** about the accuracy of answers is essential to permanent learning. Peeking ahead at the back of the book does not teach us anything.

1) What keyboard shortcut reverses our last PPT command?
2) How many (maximum) commands can we cancel in PPT?
3) We can NOT cancel which two File Menu commands in PPT?
4) Which hand should we use for keyboard shortcuts?
    a. Left hand   b. Right hand
    c. Either left or right   d. Both left and right
5) When we click inside a text placeholder it is selected:
    a. Slanted border lines   b. Checkered border lines
    c. For moving   d. For total replacement
6) When you click inside a text placeholder then hit your "Escape key" the text box is selected how:
    a. Slanted border lines   b. Checkered border lines
    c. For editing only
7) The best MS Design Template© to use is
    a. A template with medium shades
    b. One that has artwork on every slide
    c. One with artistic "shadow" font
    d. Don't use any MS Design Template©.
8) On the first rectangular array of color choices, click on
    a. A Dark color rectangle
    b. A Medium color rectangle
    c. A Light color rectangle
    d. "More Colors…" under the rectangular choices
9) On the hexagonal color wheel, where can we find the following?
    a. a Dark color –
    b. a Light color -
    c. a Medium color –
10) Medium shades should never be used __ a text box placeholder.
    a. Inside   b. Outside
    c. On top of   d. In Word Art© creations in
11) The default (automatic) FILL COLOR in PPT text placeholders is __.
    a. Dark   b. Light   c. Medium   d. None (transparent)
12) What is the keyboard combination for formatting the font in a text placeholder?

13) Should we make all text Shadow special effect so it will look 3-D?

14) What is the keyboard shortcut for adding border lines around text placeholders?

15) How do we change the color of one whole slide's background?

16) What keyboard shortcut changes the fill color in a text placeholder?

17) List 5 choices that make text boxes legible.

a

b

c

d

e

18) When does boldfacing a font make it more legible?
a. Always   b. Sometimes   c. Never

19) Do we need headings/titles on slides? (yes they are advance organizers)
(End of Open Book Test One)

Summary- 6 steps that make a slide a minute

TYPE ALL THE TEXT into a word processing program, NOT into PowerPoint©.

Select all the Word text. Copy and paste all the text into the OUTLINE TAB heading in the left window in Normal editing view in PowerPoint©.

Then use these commands:

Enter Key = a new line at the same indent level. Make a first pass through all slides using Enter to form slides. Just chop it into slides on the first pass. Do NOT make the bulleted items yet.

Tab Key = demotes new slide to bullet (moves right) Wait to do this until the second pass in Outline View, until all slides have been visited and are defined with the Enter Key in Outline View. Shift + Tab works the reverse way.

After two passes through Outline view, Shift with Tab in Outline Tab heading converts bullets to new slide (moves text to the left)

For any line that does not look right? Backspace the first word until it merges with the line above. Hit the Enter Key to break them apart again; it will behave now.

---

30 Slides In 30 Minutes Concept Map

No other technique can make 30 text slides in 30 minutes.

Typing the same text in a different place and learning some keyboard shortcuts is the key. The keyboard shortcut knowledge is transferable since identical Outline controls were provided in MS Powerpoint© and MS Word©.

Most students report it would take them two days or 16 hours to create 30 bulleted text slides. Very few presenters know how to save 15 of those 16 hours. Read this section with MS Word© and Powerpoint already open.

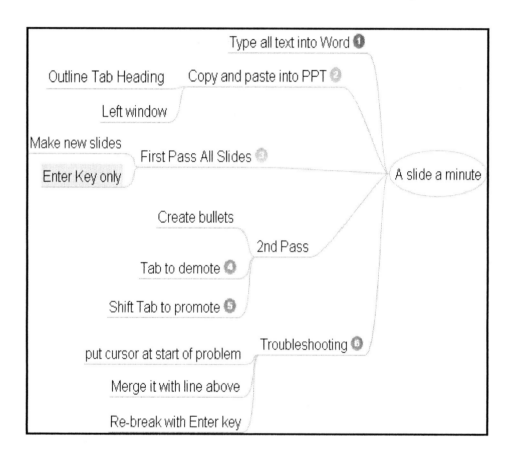

Choose the Right Tool

Most students when asked if they can type 30 wpm reply "Yes." If our goal is to put a lot of words into a program fast we will choose Wordperfect, Sun Office Write (free to students and convertible to Word) or MS Word. Typing into text placeholders is a time consuming habit and there is no way to approach your word processor speed in the PPT placeholders. There is a way to average a slide per minute though.

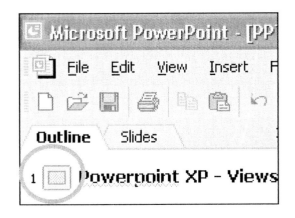

1.) Paste all the text (Ctrol A, Ctrol C, Ctrol V) in the Outline tab heading on the left window pane. See illustration left.
It will all go into the title placeholder of slide one.

Make the Outline Tab heading wider, until the middle editing window looks like a postage stamp.

The left window can be made bigger in Outline tab than it can in Slides tab. The left pane has two tabs, the default Slides tab and the timesaving Outline tab. Put the blinking cursor to the right of "slide numbered 1" in the left window.

Widen the left pane by placing the cursor on its vertical boundary line and left-dragging it toward the right. The mouse pointer becomes a 2-headed arrow when it can resize an object.

When the left pane is widened it shrinks the center normal or editing pane.

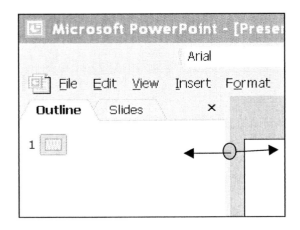 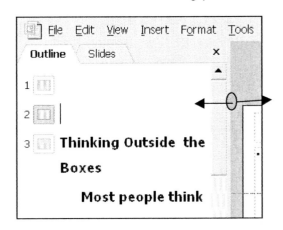

All the imported text is in the title of one slide!

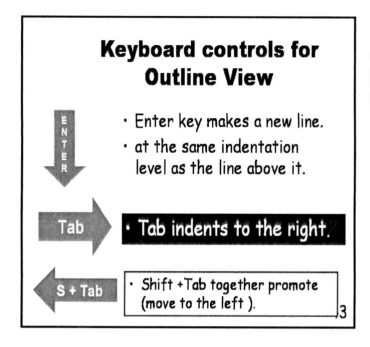

A slide (reproduced left) shows what the 3 keyboard controls do, while in the Outline Tab heading in PPT. Refer to it often or memorize it.

First Pass: Create New Slides

2.) Make a first pass through all slides and ONLY use the Enter key to make new slides, completely ignoring bullets. Use Control +Z to undo mistakes. The slide below says Enter gives a new line at the same indentation level the cursor was at. We were at the slide title level so we get new slides with the Enter key.

Second Pass: Make Bullets

3.) Then on the second visit to every slide repeat this two step sequence:

3.A.) To make the first bullet following a slide title, hit the Enter key then the Tab key. Enter then Tab turns on automatic bullet formatting

3.B.) To make the 2nd through last bullets on the same slide use only the Enter key not the Tab key. We were at the bullet level; we get another bullet at the same indentation spot.

3.C.) Avoid second and deeper indentation level bullets. They are hard to read and cause a show to drag. Remove them from the Master Slide.

Troubleshooting Tip

4.) There is a single troubleshooting tip needed to complete the tool kit. There will be places that don't look right and seem resistant to change. Here's the tip:

4.A.) Put the cursor at the beginning of the line that looks wrong.

4.B.) Merge it with the line above. The Delete key or Backspace key accomplish this.

4.C.) Break the lines with the Enter Key. The obstinate line will behave.

30 Slides in 30 Minutes - Review

Summary – Outline Tab Controls

- Get all the text into MS Word© or www.OpenOffice.org's "Write" (free to students and convertible to Word) or into a WordPerfect from Corel file.
- Select it all. Copy it. Paste it into the Outline View, the left-hand window of PPT.
- Memorize these 3 keyboard controls
  - Enter = new line
  - Tab = move text to right
  - Shift + Tab = move text to left
- Use the keyboard shortcuts shown above to chop it
  - into slides on the first pass and
  - bullets on the second pass.
- Merge and then re-break lines where problems start.
- Nothing replaces practice. Make the first 30 slides in 30 minutes this way. Typing all the words into text place holders in PPT, would take hours and hours.

One troubleshooting procedure

If it looks wrong anywhere, go to the first place it looks wrong. Use the delete key or the backspace key to make that trouble spot merge with the line above it in Outline Tab. Then do ENTER, and either TAB or Shift Tab. Merging then re-breaking the lines is all one needs to know.

The four tips above should be memorized. What do you get in return? You can create the text part of slide shows in 75% less time by typing in Outline Tab Heading and avoiding typing into text placeholders on the slides

MS PPT 2007© Keyboard Shortcuts

Ctrl + mouse wheel	Zoom in or Zoom out
Ctrl + [	decrease font size one next step lower
Ctrl +]	Increase font size one next step higher
Ctrl + A	All content selected
Ctrl + B	Bold Text
Ctrl + C	Copy
Ctrl + D	Duplicate Object in Place
Ctrl + E	Center align
Ctrl + F	Find- also Replace
Ctrl + G	Go to (in MS Word); turn Guides on (PPT)
Ctrl + I	Italic
Ctrl + J	Justify fully – both sides
Ctrl + K	Insert Hyperlink
Ctrl + L	Left align
Ctrl + M	More Slides (Insert slide)
Ctrl + N	New File
Ctrl + O	Open File
Ctrl + P	**Print** (normal view); **Pen** (slide show view)
Ctrl + Q	Quit (PPT)
Ctrl + R	Right align
Ctrl + S	Save
Ctrl + T	Format the fonT
Ctrl + U	Underline
Ctrl + V	Paste (looks like an arrow head)
Ctrl + X	Cut (looks like scissors)
Ctrl + Y	Repeat Previous Action
Ctrl + Z	Undo Previous Action

Designing Slide Titles

Information Organizer

Each slide must have a title placeholder filled out. It is a valuable information organizer which summarizes a slide's content with a few keywords. All the words and images on a slide relate to the brief title. The title plays the role of a scaffold for hanging the new knowledge in a place so that is easy to retrieve. **Descriptive titles make the key points easier to recall after the show is over**.

Describes Contents

A slide title needs to describe the contents not merely be cute. That requires a keyword or two, other times a very short sentence.

Hyperlink, Preview, Summary, Navigation

Comprehension only one reason for using every Title Placeholder. Having a title on every slide makes hyperlinks easier to find and work with. Titles let you create labor-saving automated Preview and Summary slides. They speed up the time to make a first draft.

Hiding a Title

If we do not want the title to show on a certain slide? Make the title font the same color as the slide background and it disappears in Normal View, but shows up in the Outline View pane in the left window pane.

Bigger than body text & more noticeable

One rule of designing Titles is: headings should attract more attention than the bulleted or body text. Some make Titles larger. Try using a font face such as Arial Black in the slide title. Arial Black "throws a lot of ink" onto a slide. A 40 point Arial Black title can thus command more attention than a 54 point body text font of just plain Arial.

Strategy 1:   A title should describe that slide's content.
Strategy 2:   A title should be brief.
Strategy 3:   Some authors use one or two keywords.

Never animate title placeholders

Slide one is an exception. A title placeholder should only be animated on a single slide, which is the first slide of the show, nowhere else. Interestingly, the first slide is often the only slide where a medium or a slow custom animation speed looks natural. It is one of only two slides where the custom animation named "Credits" makes sense, the other location being the final slide. The audience has probably seen enough movies to expect the first or last frame to be prolonged.

Blank slide, blank mind

Custom Animation on *bulleted text boxes* prevents cluttered slides, gains attention, and enhances audience retention and recall. Animating bulleted text makes much sense. But when *title placeholders* receive custom animation the presentation suffers.

When we first arrive at a slide whose title is animated, what do we see? Nothing. How does such a blank screen cue our memory of the extra points we wanted to make? A blank screen also gives our audience blank minds and it makes them impatient. Recall that a title should be 1) brief and should 2) describe the contents of that slide. If we also draw a blank, we may lose our sharpness and command of the material. Any features not animated display immediately when the slide first appears. Therefore, *never animate the title placeholders after slide one.*

Nearly all custom animated objects should be created with either a fast or very fast speed setting. *No audience seems to like a slow custom animation.* Custom animations simply have to "rock." The one place audiences do expect to see slower motion is on the first or Title Slide of a show, or credits scrolling across the last slide. Perhaps this expectation comes from watching movies.

Open-Book Test 2 Placeholders

1) Each slide's title placeholder is a valuable information what? _____ which summarizes a slide's content with keywords.
2) A slide title needs to _____ not merely be cute.
3) One fast way to come up with a header is start the first part of a sentence in the header or title placeholder and _____.
4) Three features in PPT will not work well without having a title on every slide. Two of these are Automatic Preview and Summary slides in Slide Sorter View. Another is H _____ (hint: starts with H)
5) (T/F) Headings must be 12 points larger than the body text. True or False?
6) (T/F) Titles should be centered and stretch across the top of a slide. True or False?.
7) (T/F) A 36-point font is the same physical size whether in Times New Roman font , Arial Black, or Comic Sans MS. True or False?
8) A title should be:
9)   a. Detailed   b. 36 points   c. Descriptive   d. bold faced
10)A title serves as a one-slide _____.
11)   a. URL   b. organizer   c. ending   d. navigator
12) When a title placeholder is selected All, for moving or changing all the contents at once, what is the border like?
              a. Slanted lines   b. Checkered lines
13)   c. marching ants   d. dotted
14) If title text is highlighted or selected, and we hold the Control Key while striking several times on the right (]) square parenthesis key (just above the E in the Enter Key) what happens?
              a. Changes Case   b. switches font
15)   c. Changes Alignment   d. Grows
16) Shift and the F3 (function 3) key cycles through 3 types of case. Which three?
_____   _____   _____
17) _____ case capitalizes every major word but not articles (a, an, or the) nor short prepositions. Prepositions of 5 or more letters are capitalized. (Hint: starts with a "t," and has shortcut Shift+ F3)
18) To change the case of all title placeholders on every subsequent new slide, we have to change it on the Slide M_____ (hint: starts with M)
19) (T/F) ALL CAPS IS A GOOD CHOICE FOR TITLES SINCE IT IS SO LEGIBLE. True or False?
20) (T/F) Title Placeholders should never be animated except possibly on the first Title Slide? True or False?
21) Custom animation should be used on all
22)   a. Titles   b. Bullets   c. slides   d. bullets with sound
23) Title Placeholders can be aligned left, right or center from the keyboard. What is the shortcut to Center a title? _____
24)
25) Title placeholders by default, are centered horizontally and vertically which means as a new title line appears, text scrolls up not down. How do we fix that to scroll down only? Part of the answer is provided, complete it below.
26) "To change the scrolling behavior select the title placeholder, and on the menu bar choose Format, Placeholder." Then what? _____

End of self-test 2.

Custom Animation

-- "The most fun you can have on campus with your clothes on"

AVOID "animation schemes"

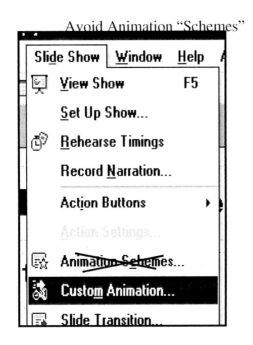

There are two animation choices in PowerPoint©. One to avoid is Slide Show, "animation schemes."

Audiences do not like reading moving text, cluttered bulleted list boxes, or waiting for titles to appear. Yes, animation schemes even animate titles. Many of the "schemes" are slow.

Microsoft© is not qualified to make such decisions. Any audience will want to leave as single letters fall one by one into a title placeholder.

CHOOSE "Slide show, custom animation"

The second pathway for animations is "Slide show, custom animation."

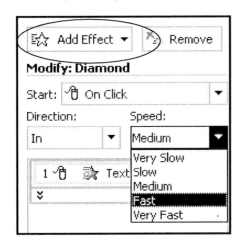

After Slide Show, Custom Animation, select a text object or a graphic object to animate.

Click once on the image. That selects the object, and displays tiny resizing handles.

Click on the "Add Effect" button, circled on the upper left.

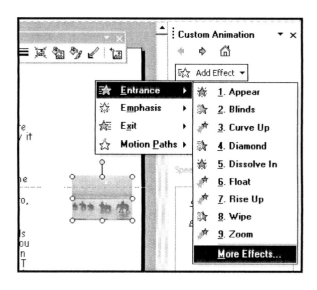

The screen print on the left has a photo of elephants. It is selected on a slide.

The Add Effect list box button is open. In order of appearance, are Entrance, Emphasis, and Exit. Choose "Entrance."

Choose "More Effects..." the last one. The list has up to 9 other recently used effects.

Animation Sequence: Title, Photo, Text

So far we have seen titles serve an I.T. purpose as advance organizers and they need to appear on all slides. But *when* should they appear?

There are three major fields on most slides:

title placeholder,

graphic image,

and a bulleted text placeholder.

The menu choices Slide Show, then Custom Animation, chronologically sequences their appearance with user selected animation effects. You must determine the best sequence.

The most EFFECTIVE sequence, according to cognitive psychologists and instructional technologists, is: Do NOT animate the title placeholder at all. This means the title appears first before any animations occur. It is an Advance Organizer for the words on the slide.

Avoid the temptation to skip using a title. EVERY slide needs a title, even if we have to hide it by making it the same color as the slide background. As we design a new show, we can read the titles in the Outline View of the left window pane in Powerpoint©. If we hyperlink to a slide it saves time to have all slides titled.

If we animate any titles then we come upon "blank" slides, at least until we advance the animation timings by clicking. Our minds will briefly go blank. It disorients our audience. If the first thing we see on a slide is its title, we have a brief, descriptive advance organizer instead of a blank.

- Tough time making hyperlinks.
- No way to use time-saving
  Outline View in the left window.
- No way to do automated previews
  or summaries.
- No organizer for that one slide.

Graphics precede bulleted text

Animate graphic images to appear before bulleted text. Graphic images relieve an audience of having to form all their own mental pictures for what we are saying. Graphics are also Advance Organizers. If graphics appear after the bulleted text, it is too late for them to do their job effectively.

Use Google Image Search© and type in keywords for finding relevant clip art, photos, and animated GIFs. Attempt to put one image on every slide. Vary the size and position of graphics. Vary the position of titles within the show. Then animate the bulleted text to appear after the photos.

titles are never animated

Consider what we want the audience to see as we present a bulleted list called a "text and title" auto layout. When the slide appears the title should be already visible because it functions as an advance organizer. Ensure the title appears first, by not animating the title placeholder at all.

Text that flies across, spirals through, or slams into a margin and falls backward are distractions from the message and annoy an audience. So does "Crawl In" effect and medium speed or slower.

Animate lists to appear one bullet at a time

Bulleted text should be animated so it doesn't appear all at once. Cognitive psychologists call this chunking. Animated bullets prevent visual clutter & cognitive (memory) overload. Animated bullets gain our attention and focus it. When sequence or relative ranking is important within a list, bulleted lists can be numbered to show the priority.

Animate Text – Basic category; very fast

Add Entrance Effect

The "Add Entrance Effect" list box groups effects into categories.

The category "Basic" lists 19 effects. All 19 share one feature: compatibility with older versions of the software. By sheer coincidence, 16 of the 19 are excellent for animating **bulleted text**.

The "Basic" list starts the text already in its final resting position. Good. The text is motionless but reveals itself in some pattern. Better.

Moving text bores an audience. So does slow animation speeds.

Work at home - To take the file home and work on it in an older version of MS PowerPoint©, use only Basic category animations. They are compatible with older versions of PPT (are supported).Add an effect to text

Text that moves at all irritates an audience. So do slow animations. **All animations should be very fast or fast.**

Most listed in the category Basic are great for text.

Do not pick
Crawl In (too slow)
Fly In (moves).
Random Effects
(both problems).

Choose only Very Fast or Fast speed, in the 16 Basic effects.

Design rules that "random effects" (see above) violate are: revealed in place, no motion, and speed ought to be very fast or fast.

Nearly all custom animations should be very fast. If very fast looks bad, the next choice is fast. **There are 3 speeds for animation: very fast, fast, and lost your audience.** "Dude, animations have to rock!"

Animating a Bulleted Box

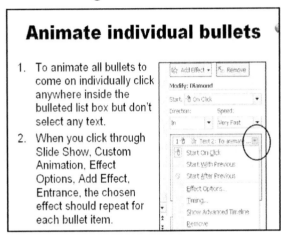

To animate a bulleted text box, do not select it All (with a checkered border) or we can't show bullets one at a time easily.

Click inside the text field once. The border has slanted lines. Bullets enter one at a time.

We can only see a slanted line border if the mouse cursor is blinking. A blinking cursor (or a cursing blinker) is the visual signal we need here.

Troubleshooting Multiple Bullets

If more than one bullet arrives on a slide at once, hit the REMOVE effect button and re-select the bulleted text with a blinking cursor (slanted border). When you re-select, but more than bullet arrives on the same mouse click, click the arrow head on the right of the selected item (the bulleted box).Pick the choice Effect Options... which is below the separator line of the drop down menu.

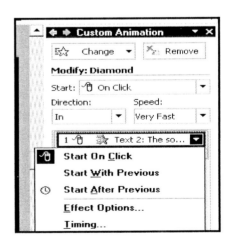

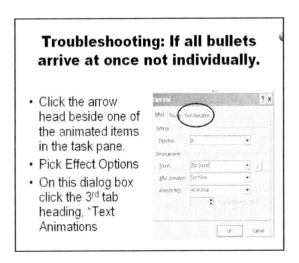

Select the 3rd tab heading, "**Text Animations**." Scroll down the list box under "Group text" and select "**By 1st level paragraphs**." Now the bullets should appear one at a time. See the figure below left.

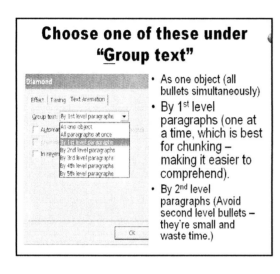

Choose one of these under "Group text"

- As one object (all bullets simultaneously)
- By 1st level paragraphs (one at a time, which is best for chunking – making it easier to comprehend).
- By 2nd level paragraphs (Avoid second level bullets – they're small and waste time.)

Suppose we want 1 bullet not animated, the other 2 animated?

We would select by highlighting with the mouse only bullets #2 and #3.

When we go through the menu choices Slide Show, Custom Animation only the pre-selected bullets (2 & 3) will be animated.

To remove animations

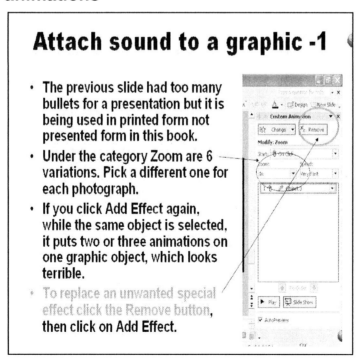

Attach sound to a graphic -1

- The previous slide had too many bullets for a presentation but it is being used in printed form not presented form in this book.
- Under the category Zoom are 6 variations. Pick a different one for each photograph.
- If you click Add Effect again, while the same object is selected, it puts two or three animations on one graphic object, which looks terrible.
- To replace an unwanted special effect click the Remove button, then click on Add Effect.

Animating graphics

Any animation is fine on *graphic objects* when the speed is very fast.

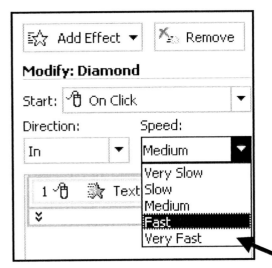

Select inside a bulleted list box. On the menu click Slide Show, Custom Animation, then the buttons Add Effect, On Entrance, More Effects... (Look at the **Basic** list.)

Speed: very fast, or fast. Choose a very fast animation that reveals the text in a shape (box, diamond, dissolve, circle, etc.).

Adult audiences dislike text that either dive-bombs the slide or arrives slowly. Graphic images may fly around; text should not.

Under BASIC, the Diamond effect is medium speed by default. Increase the speed and it is usable for text.

Color, Font, Animatiom- Concept Map

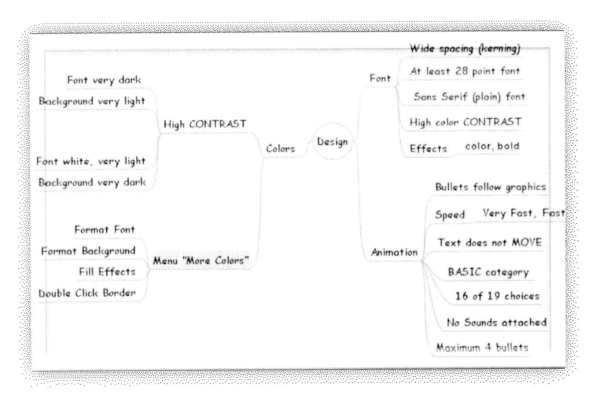

Speed- Very Fast, Fast, Lost the Audience...

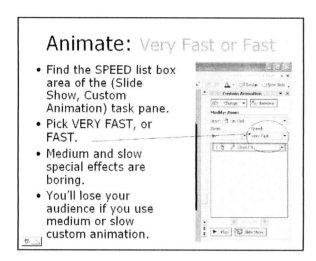

Animate: Very Fast or Fast

- Find the SPEED list box area of the (Slide Show, Custom Animation) task pane.
- Pick VERY FAST, or FAST.
- Medium and slow special effects are boring.
- You'll lose your audience if you use medium or slow custom animation.

Some "Basic" effects such as Diamond are revealed in a pattern and do not fly around the screen, but they have a slow speed.

Diamond effect is set for medium. The audience is set for very fast. What's wrong with this picture?

In the animation order task pane, change the speed to very fast.

Animating Photos, Embedding Camera Sound

For clip art, any category of custom animation is usable. For text, use the Basic category of animation effects except for Fly In, Crawl In and Random Effects.

For photographs, try some of six variations of the Zoom effect under the category "Moderate." Embed the sound of a clicking shutter, so when the photograph zooms, the audience hears a camera click. Use a camera sound that comes with Powerpoint©.

Embedding sound into a photo or image is invaluable to a designer of slide shows. It beats discovering your sounds won't play on presentation day. The chapter on sounds goes into details on this topic. Where it originated was when not many people had enough RAM memory to run PPT. Programmers designed PPT to link sound files above a small limit instead of embedding them. When a person presents on a different computer than they created the show with, they need to place their sound files in the same folder as their dot PPT file or they won't play. Embedding sounds is done on the Effect Options settings in the Slide Show, Custom Animation task pane. It requires an animated graphic to trigger the sound, but it is always reliable.

To Custom Animate a Photo -1

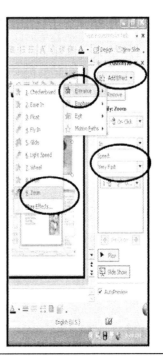

1. Select (click once on) the picture.
2. **Slide Show, Custom Animation.**
3. In the right task pane window click the button "**Add Effect**."
4. Click on **Entrance**.
5. Click **More Effects** and find **Zoom**.
6. **Choose any variation of zoom, but make the speed only very fast or fast.**
7. Slow animations lose an audience.
8. Zoom looks very good on photos.
9. The next slide tells how to add a prerecorded sound such as **the sound of a camera** shutter to the photo.

This seems irrelevant, but is truly vital. Before we make sounds play reliably in Powerpoint©, we have to animate a graphic object then we embed the sound in that graphic. Step one is above. Zoom is merely one animation subcategory suggestion. Any animation effect will play if embedded in the graphic

.

To clear animations and restart-1

Attach sound to a graphic -1

- The previous slide had too many bullets for a presentation but it is being used in printed form not presented form in this book.
- Under the category Zoom are 6 variations. Pick a different one for each photograph.
- If you click Add Effect again, while the same object is selected, it puts two or three animations on one graphic object, which looks terrible.
- To replace an unwanted special effect click the Remove button, then click on Add Effect.

Start with a custom animated photo (see above.)

Embed sound in a graphic-2

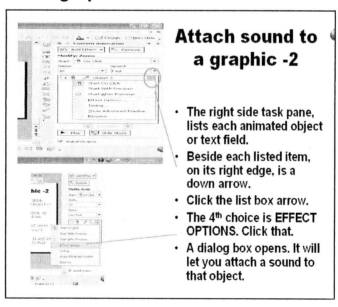

Attach sound to a graphic -2

- The right side task pane, lists each animated object or text field.
- Beside each listed item, on its right edge, is a down arrow.
- Click the list box arrow.
- The 4th choice is EFFECT OPTIONS. Click that.
- A dialog box opens. It will let you attach a sound to that object.

Embed any sound in an image.

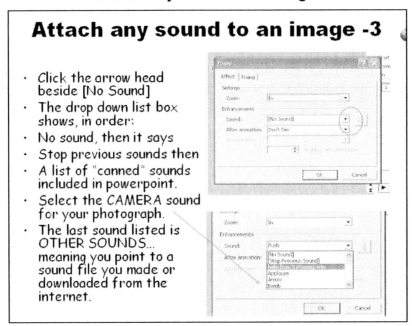

Attach any sound to an image -3

- Click the arrow head beside [No Sound]
- The drop down list box shows, in order:
- No sound, then it says
- Stop previous sounds then
- A list of "canned" sounds included in powerpoint.
- Select the CAMERA sound for your photograph.
- The last sound listed is OTHER SOUNDS... meaning you point to a sound file you made or downloaded from the internet.

Organization of Effect Options, Sounds

Click on Effect Options. Change its dialog box from No Sounds to Camera. The list begins with No Sounds then Stop Previous Sound.

Next, in chronological order are recently made sounds using the menu choices Insert, Movies and Sounds, Record Sound.

Following the chronological list is an alphabetized list of sound effects including camera and applause. These are prerecorded sounds within PPT and come with the software. Choose the camera click and hit OK.

The last choice at the bottom of the list is Other Sounds... It's the menu choice for downloaded sounds from the internet or from a CD or a USB Memory Stick. We currently recommend the website **www.Findsounds.com** for sound effects.

Embed our voice in a photograph

To create a recording of our voice within PPT click the menu choices Insert, Movies and Sounds, RECORD SOUND (not "sound from file").

Use MS Powerpoint® as a Tape Recorder. Plug in a microphone to the jack labeled with a microphone symbol, or to the red jack in the back of the computer. If the microphone has an on-off switch then turn it on.

Click on the menu choices Insert, Movie or Sound, RECORD SOUND , the last choice. The tiny recording window looks like a simple tape recorder. Notice the arrowhead play button, then a stop recording square, and a red ball to begin recording.

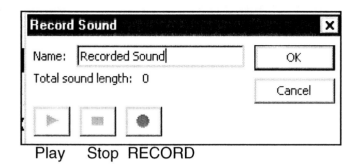

Play   Stop   RECORD

We change the name of each sound to something that describes the contents of the file.

In case we do record several sounds all named "Recorded Sound" the most recent one will be listed first in the Effect Options dialog boxes.

First change the file name but don't hit the OK button. Otherwise, all recordings will be blank and be named "Recorded Sound." Strangely, these sounds are allowed the same name and can exist separately in the same list! The one at the top of the list is the most recent.

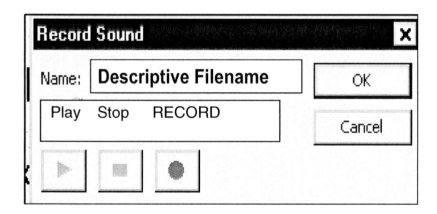

Don't accidentally hit the OK button- there's nothing in the sound file to save yet (Total sound length: 0).

Practice. Hold the microphone 1-2 inches from your lips and hit the red-ball button to start recording.

Take a breath right now so the first words are not cut off. Speak loudly and clearly. When you're done, count three in your head to not chop off sound, and then hit the black rectangle button that stops recording. Practice until it sounds friendly. If the recording is not a keeper hit the "Cancel" button and go through the menus again. When the recording is good, hit the "OK" button to save and name it.

Embed a recording in an animated graphic.

Animate the graphic, and select it. Notice it is also selected in the right task pane, in the order of animations. Whichever item it is, click the selected arrow head beside that item on its right edge.

Embed internet sound effects in a photograph

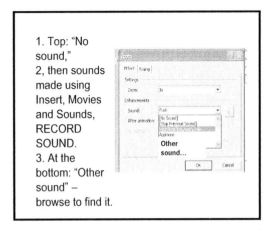

1. Top: "No sound,"
2, then sounds made using Insert, Movies and Sounds, RECORD SOUND.
3. At the bottom: "Other sound" – browse to find it.

The last choice in the list is "Other sounds..."

Use it to find sound effects downloaded from the internet or use it to locate sounds recorded but not in PPT itself.

This step EMBEDS the sound IN THE OBJECT. It will play reliably on presentation day.

Sounds can be added to a graphic with the Effect Options menu choices shown above. Then they will play reliably. Sounds should not be added to bulleted list boxes because the repeated sound is irritating.

Never add sounds to a bulleted list!

- The sound will play several times in a row.
- The second time it becomes stale.
- The fourth time it is quite irritating.
- There is no requirement to have bulleted text on all slides.
- Use it as you need it.
- Bulleted lists & tables present technical information better than plain paragraphs.

The slide to the left has a reminder that sounds should be embedded in graphics, but not in bulleted text boxes.

Warning! Put screeching brakes on 1 of 6 bullets, and it will play 6 times not once. Do so on the Master Slide and it plays on every mouse click in the whole show! Won't that tarnish your image?

Selected animation effects.

Wipe effect is located under the Basic category in the More Effects task pane. It can be used with text but the default direction is Wipe, Up. Modify it to Wipe, From Left. It looks more natural.

Wipe effect is ideal for animating a pointing line or an arrow. It makes lines seem to be drawn by an invisible hand. Attach the sound of an arrow (twang!) from Findsounds.com. Wipe is excellent for showing sequences.

Bounce & Light Speed are intended to be humorous and look better at Medium Speed. Very few other effects look good at that medium speed.

Pinwheel & Sling & Swivel will make you look like a clown.

Only Animations from the **Basic category** belong on text. Three exceptions are Crawl In, Fly In, and Random Effects.

Open Book Test 3-Animation Design

Please take the following self-test as an open book test.

1. Which option gives more control over animations: Custom Animation or Animation Schemes?

2. It is optional whether to type in the title placeholder. (True or false?)

3. What are two advantages to animating bulleted lists?

4. You should embed sounds in a bulleted list to reduce boredom? (T/F)

5. What is the "First rule of software"?

6. Which speed should you use (slow / medium / fast / very fast?) to animate bulleted text.

7. To animate a bulleted list box, what selection pattern should the list box border show, slanted lines or checkered?

8. Select one best animation for bulleted text from only these 4 choices:
   a. Slow, diamond,   b. Fast, fly in,
   c. Medium, spiral in   d. Very Fast, circle

9. To make a photo more dramatic use Pinwheel or Swivel effect (T/F)

10 Only effects listed under Basic should go with text. (T/F)

11 Any effect listed under Basic should go with text. (T/F)

12 Text should randomly fly in but at slow speed. (T/F)

13 Which effect makes lines and arrows appear to be drawn by an invisible hand?

14 It is not possible to animate only the 2nd and 3rd bullets, skipping animating the 1st one in a box with 3 bulleted items. (T/F).

15 Bulleted text should always be animated, with a fast or very fast speed, and from the Basic category. (T/F)

16. Photographs should be animated to appear after bulleted text. (T/F)

17. Title placeholders are optional and should be animated fast or very fast. (T/F)

18. The technology used in a slide show should be remembered after the words are long forgotten. (T/F)

19. It is fine for all bullets to appear at once. (T/F)

20. If all bullets appear at once then one should look under Effect Options, but which tab heading?

SOUNDS

There are several ways to put sounds into MS Powerpoint® but only a few play reliably. Create and practice a presentation on one computer, but give the show on a different computer, sounds won't play. Sound files must be in the same folder as the slide show's ".PPT" file at the moment you first link them, and once again when you perform your slide show. This unit teaches how to embed sounds in graphics so they play reliably.

Change 2003 default settings

to make PPT friendlier. Change **1)** makes Powerpoint embed larger sound files (so they play reliably). The file size will grow but it's well worth it. Change **2)** shows more files on the recent file list at the bottom of the file menu. Change **3)** shows full menus immediately, without that annoying delay.

Changes needed in PPT© 2003 only

Change the recently used file list: to show the maximum, 9 files. Then hit the OK button.

Click the menu bar on **Tools, Options**, select the General Tab. Change the "Link sounds with file size greater than 100 KB" to read "2000 KB." It embeds sounds within PPT unless the sound is more than 2 Megabytes

Click the menu choices **Tools, Customize**. Click the Options Tab and click to put a check mark beside "Always show full menus." It also works in other MS Office© software.

Where do sound files belong?

Please notice the location significance of sounds. If they aren't in the slide show's folder when they are connected, and yet again when played, don't expect them to work on the day you present. Move all sounds into the PPT show's same folder BEFORE you try to put the sound into Powerpoint. When you have a choice of formats choose dot WAV (*.wav).

Why reliable means embedded

MS Powerpoint® only embeds Narrations. It unreliably links other sound files to the presentation file. When you think you are putting a sound "into" the presentation, you're not. You're putting a pointer called a link inside your show. To keep the presentation from growing very large, the sounds you put "in to Powerpoint®" don't actually go anywhere, least of all "in to Powerpoint©." That's why we changed the PPT© 2003 menu to embed sounds up to 2 megabytes within Powerpoint© (Tools, Customize, General Tab, change 100 KB to 2000 KB).

We regain reliability once we embed sounds into animated graphic objects. We use the Effect Options tab in the Custom Animation Task Pane to embed sounds.

Map: Images & (Embedded) Sounds

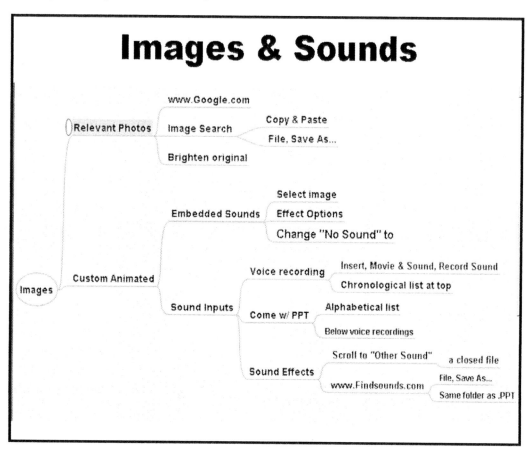

Embedding sounds in 4 steps

We will 1) insert a graphic, 2) animate that graphic, 3) create a voice sound, then 4) embed the recorded sound in the graphic using Effect Options. It will play reliably.

1) Place a graphic object on a slide.

If Powerpoint® is open, copy some legal image, then paste it onto a slide. Or, use "Insert, Picture, From File..." and point to the picture in the browse window. Fill in the menu top to bottom. To use the Insert menu, the image must be closed.

2) Animate it,

choosing Slide Show, Custom Animation.
Select that graphic we just inserted or pasted.
Choose Add an Effect, On Entrance, and choose one of the fun animation effects. Animating objects is the most fun you have with your clothes on at work or school. Now we have a slide with an animated graphic. Next we

(3) Record or download a sound,

(4) Then embed the sound in the animated graphic object.

Insert, Media Clips, Sound, Record Sound - PPT© 2007

Plug in a microphone to the jack labeled with a microphone symbol, the red jack of the computer. If the microphone has an on-off switch, turn it on.

Click on the Home menu choice Insert, find the ribbon tab heading Media Clips on the right, choose SOUND.

This drop down list appears.

To record your voice while in PowerPoint © 2007 pick the last choice, **Record Sound.**

The tiny recording window looks like a simple tape recorder. Notice the arrow-head play button, then a stop recording square, and a red ball to begin recording.

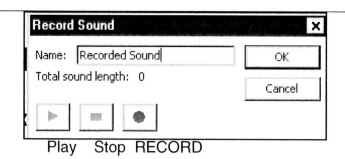

Play   Stop   RECORD

Change the name of each sound to something that describes the contents of the file, but **don't hit the OK button.**

Otherwise, all recordings will be blank and be named "Recorded Sound."

Strangely, these sounds are allowed the same name in the same list! The one at the top of the list is the most recent. Call our sound "three reasons" or anything that describes the contents well.

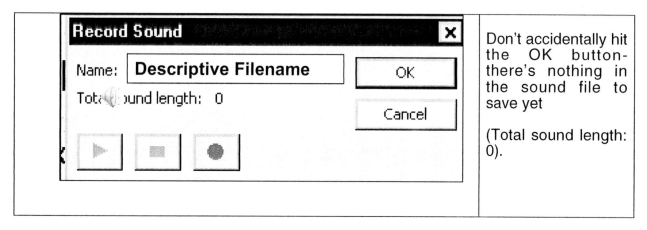

Don't accidentally hit the OK button- there's nothing in the sound file to save yet

(Total sound length: 0).

Practice until it sounds friendly. Hold the microphone 3-4 inches from your lips and hit the red-ball button to start recording. Take a breath right now so the first words are not cut off. Speak loudly and clearly. When done, count three to not chop off sound, and then hit the black rectangle button that stops recording. **Practice until it sounds friendly**. Do not try to imitate Hollywood announcers.

If the recording is not a keeper hit the "Cancel" button and go through the menus again. When the recording is good, hit the "OK" button to save and name it.

4) Embed a recording in an animated graphic.

Animate the graphic, and select it. Notice it is also selected in the right task pane, in the order of animations. Whichever item it is, **click the arrow head beside that selected item on its right edge.**

Custom Animation Pane

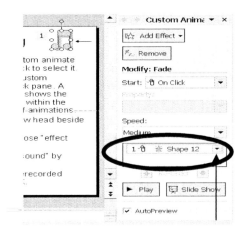

Find the selected graphic on the slide (left). The white circles, called resizing handles, tell us it's selected.

When we click on Slide Show, Custom Animation, a task pane opens right of the slide. See the numbered order, what sequence it will appear. There is a "1" to the left of it. Look inside the oval (left).

Click the **down arrowhead** (_) at the right side of the highlighted item.

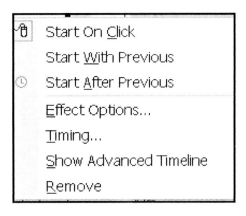

A shortcut menu (left) appears. Click **"Effect Options." Click it.**

The next dialog box lets you add sounds or voices, change an animation's timing, and make bulleted lists come on one bullet a time (desirable) or all at once (not best).

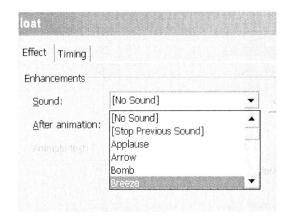

On the Effect Options... dialog box, **change the Sound field** from [No Sound] to a sound on the scrollable list.

At the top is a chronological list of the recent sounds and voices we recorded.

Our recently created sound will be found near the top of the chronological list, above Applause.

PPT prerecorded sounds.

The two problems with prerecorded sounds are 1) there aren't enough of them and 2) choosing sounds that are unrelated to your topic and also aren't funny.

Prerecorded Effect Options

Which visual object is related to a camera sound? Photographs. Watch 100 slide shows- you won't see many photographs animated or embedded with a camera shutter sound. Yours will be special.

Put a photo on a practice slide using **Insert, Picture, From File...** A graphic file must be **closed** before it can be inserted.

Click once on the photo to select it.
In the Custom Animation Task Pane on the right side:

Click on Slide Show, Custom animation, Add Effect, On Entrance,
    Scroll down to **More Choices**.
    Choose **Zoom** in the "Moderate" area, & OK.

In the animation task pane (shown on your left) click to modify Zoom further.

There are 6 zoom effects.
Try them out and choose one.
Next, embed the camera sound in the animated graphic.

(In from screen center- place the photo away from the center.)

To add prerecorded sounds, select the photograph and click the arrow head beside it in the animation task pane.
Choose Effect Options.
Scroll to **camera** and select it.

Internet sounds

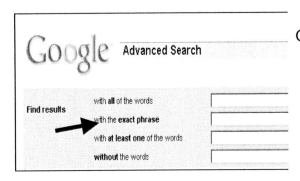

The next two sections deal with "Effect Options, **Other Sounds...**"

The sounds it applies to are:

Internet sounds such as
Findsounds.com
Google.com® (advanced search)
Windows "Sound Recorder®"

Findsounds.com

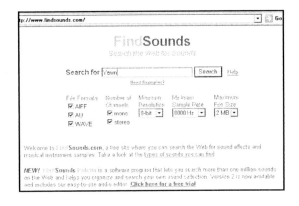

Findsounds.com has an extensive library, search box, is free, has its own fast internal search engine, and can filter or find several file extensions.

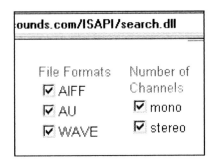

User-friendly search results are organized from smallest to largest file size. Smart. Text and graphics are switched in the next panel

Left click a speaker icon (arrows) to download and play the sound.
Save it using File, Save Media As.
Put it in your PPT show's folder and name it descriptively.

The 2nd button finds more sounds like the one previewed.

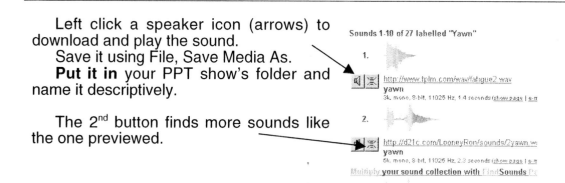

Sounds 1-10 of 27 labelled "Yawn"

1.
http://www.tplm.com/wav/fatigue2.wav
yawn
3k, mono, 8-bit, 11025 Hz, 1.4 seconds (show page | e-m

2.
http://d21c.com/LooneyRon/sounds/2yawn.w:
yawn
6k, mono, 8-bit, 11025 Hz, 2.3 seconds (show page | e-m

Multiply your sound collection with FindSounds P

Google.com advanced search for sounds

http://www.google.com/advanced_search?hl=en

A quick search for photographs on the topic "sounds" using Google's Image Search turned up 230,000 images.

This image of Tibetan healing music came from http://www.tibetanlivingcommunities.org/images/Healing%20Sounds.JPG

Find results	with **all** of the words	free sounds	100 results
	with the **exact phrase**	heart dise---	Google Search
	with **at least one** of the words	heartbeat	
	with**out** the words	xxx buy $	
Language	Return pages written in	any language	
File Format	Only return results of the file format	any format	
Date	Return web pages updated in the	anytime	
Numeric Range	Return web pages containing numbers between	and	
Occurrences	Return results where my terms occur	anywhere in the page	
Domain	Only return results from the site or domain	.edu e.g. google.com, .org Mor	
SafeSearch	○ No filtering ● Filter using SafeSearch		

Our best chance to find relevant multimedia, is to think of two words that must occur together not separately. If we want to play a healthy heartbeat sound and compare it to an unhealthy heartbeat, we could type "heart disease" in the exact phrase field. We do not need to use quotation marks in Google. In recent years other search engines have changed from proprietary typed commands to filling in clearly labeled fields like Google's. Failing that search, we replace it with "normal heartbeat." It is not necessary to type "free" before "sounds." Many free sites just say "Sounds" in their banner title.

Filter Using Safe Search

This tip is for graphic images. We turn on the "Filter Using Safe Search" and then fill in the "**without the words**" field with "game buy $" to reduce returns of pornography and sales-only websites. When searching for video clips we add the word **games** to the "without" field to decrease video games hits from the returns.

The reason for listing **100 results per page** instead of 10 is psychological. Most people feel sorry for themselves after scrolling through about three pages, whether 30 or 300 hits were evaluated. The more hits per page, the finer the search.

We can only **restrict the "domain" field to one domain at a time** if we use it at all. It is best to not restrict the domain at first. If we get a huge number of hits, then we return to the advanced search site and restrict the domain. Productive academic searches might restrict the domain to dot gov for science and health topics, or dot org for social, cultural and historic topics. Dot edu is the best choice for specialized knowledge sites. Restricting domain prematurely wastes time.

If we search only ".edu" sites more medical schools and fewer scam operations appear. We might choose a dot org restriction to try for nonprofit information sources, but anyone can lie about their status. Many dot-org sites are just video stores hawking their wares. Many true nonprofit dot-org sites are staffed by volunteers who are constantly updating and sharing new information. A great example is NPR.org. Another goldmine can sometimes be found with a dot gov domain restriction. NASA, the Smithsonian Institution, the Communicable Diseases Center, NIH, and the Library of Congress are only a few of many that have enormous free resources waiting for you to investigate.

Two other tremendous resources for multimedia include **Getty.org** and **NationalGeographic.com**. To find sites more like Getty.org use the search phrase "**video archive**" or "**video library**." Substitute words like photograph or graphic or sound or animation or clip art in place of video.

NationalGeographic.com has an unbelievable collection of "**Picture of the Day**" files. Each day an unusual picture is displayed and explained. You can browse through one past year's collection in about two or three weeks. You can't view them very fast because so many of the images are inviting, compelling. A way to decide between several good pictures is to ask, "Which one shows people or creatures in motion or doing something odd?" Viewers like to figure out what the person is doing when they see such puzzles.

Other fields that are important include the last date the site was **updated**. For a recent catastrophic news event it saves much time to fill this in.

Safer surfing for internet sound effects

When you download sounds from the internet, don't open them on your computer until you've located them in My Computer or Windows Explorer, and **right clicked those files and picked "Scan with Antivirus."**

Slide Show, Record Narration

When to use Slide Show, Record Narration? If the show will be playing automatically without a human presenter, such as at an exhibit, or a conference, etc. Or so you can be heard in a large or noisy conference room.

Portable Loudspeaker & Remote Wireless Amplifier Microphone

One can increase the volume out of the projector's speakers so we don't have to yell to be heard. A wireless microphone and a portable wireless loudspeaker solve the volume problem better than narration, because we will speak naturally. Some loudspeakers (**Apollo 5400**) let you record into a cassette tape or playback a cassette. These options beat using narration.

If we narrate a whole show for a live audience it has a terrible effect. **Nobody reads like they speak**. Just listen. Most people read as if bored, even asleep. Your audience will see the hidden message. **Use it sparingly** and relieve some boredom. Overuse narration and create boredom.

Five Parts to Recording a Narration.

Overview: The five parts are: click the menu choices, cancel the microphone quality changes, designate a slide to begin narration, hit escape to end the narration, and answer (save the timings?) either way, yes or no.

Go to the first slide we will narrate aloud. Click the menu choices Slide Show, Record Narration.

Answer the first dialog box OK unless we want to adjust the quality of the microphone (we usually don't).

Answer the next dialog box "begin with current slide" instead of on the first slide.

Record the narration. Breathe in at natural breaking points (commas or periods). Speak as when you talk to a friend. Click through to any additional slides. When you're done, hit the Escape Key to end narrating for that session.

What it asks is if you want to save the timings. Answer yes. It automatically embeds the latest recording, replacing any copies made previously.

Practical tips for recording narrations

If our microphone has its own "on/off" switch, turn it on. We may record a slide show narration starting on any slide, and may skip over slides. Narration overrules previous sounds on slides. Either do not narrate a slide that has other sounds, or, don't place other sounds on a Narrated slide. When we finish one slide click through to the next one and continue. During the performance, only those slides you spoke to, have your voice. If you were quiet as you clicked through (skipped) slides, your words do not play until the right slide appears.

If you mess up just start over from the beginning and the new narration automatically replaces the previous one completely. To eliminate the only Narration completely, start another Narration and immediately hit the "escape" key. It replaces the existing one with a split second silence no one will hear.

Pause and take a breath for some commas, periods and natural breaking points. Don't talk like the announcer at a football game – you don't have interfering echoes in most conference rooms.

Try your Hollywood best only to **sound like you actually enjoy** the subject and are keenly interested. Speak like you are talking to a friend not an audience of strangers.

Listen to how clearly you pronounced the words. Never pronounce the articles "a" or "the" with long vowel sounds. When we speak the words "a good idea" we don't say "aye good idea" where aye rhymes with say. We say "uh good idea" where "uh" rhymes with love. Nobody pronounces the article "the" like thee or we. We say "thuh" like love.

Most of us record on $4.95 microphones. They don't have a preamplifier to boost voice. Project your voice like you do on a cell phone. If you speak loudly and keep the microphone about 2 inches from the lips you can be heard clearly.

If you hear the breathed consonant sounds "p" and "t" so it sounds like you're spitting, move the microphone just far enough away to stop the spitting sound.

Want to make an audience smile? Ask a small child to share some of the narration. Let a child pronounce some of the big words or confusing sentences. Audiences love it.

Windows Sound Recorder®.

Computers that use a Windows® Operating System come equipped with the Sound Recorder® software. To open it:

Click on Start, All Programs, Accessories, Multimedia, Sound Recorder.

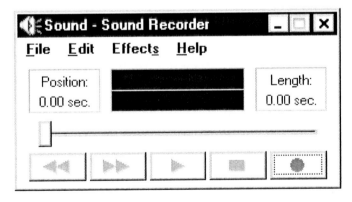

If you don't see a wave or "heartbeat" pattern as you record, one of these problems exist:

The microphone on/off switch is off.

It is on but not plugged into the computer jack.

It is plugged in to the wrong jack. The microphone input jack is red.

The microphone is defective or it is not turned on in Windows.

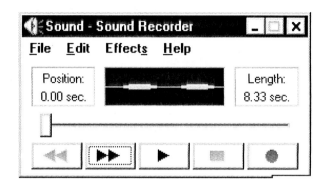

You'll see this pattern if your sound card works.

Still hear nothing on playback? It's not the input device; check the output device (head phones).

Microphone and recording tips

Hold the microphone horizontally, not vertically.

Project your voice loudly.

No audience likes slurred pronunciation or a weak voice.

Microphone horizontal

Rehearse what you'll say. Make a script or write notes.

Click the red RECORD button at the right to begin recording.

Take in a breath before you start. The split second delay prevents the program from losing the first second of speech.

Speak loudly and clearly. Pronounce the consonants, especially near the end of words. (And eat your vegetables, etc.)

When you finish, hit the stop button, the black box.

Rewind it, play it, and critique it.

If it is not great, click on File, New. Don't save the old one.

Repeat steps 2 through 5.

If it sounds great, click on File, Save As.

Place it in the folder that holds your slide show.

Name it using keywords that describe what it says.

Use the Effect Options dialog box to embed your recording in an animated graphic so it plays reliably.

Preview: The next section, has entertaining tips from students on creative ways to make recordings within Sound Recorder®.

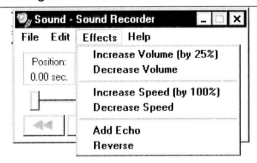

Record a sound you'll keep, such as a short introduction to the show. Say "Hi, my name is (your name). Let's talk about (your topic)." Then click on **Effects** and on **Add Echo.** Save it as "myname1.wav."

- Start a new file in Sound Recorder®. This time get a classmate or friend of the opposite gender to say the exact same words again. Due to changes in the FCC Decency Standards at the time of printing, we cannot define what opposite gender means, but you can ask an older student. Anyway, the sound of Mark's (deep) voice saying "Hi, my name is Elizabeth Garcia. Let's talk about DNA Replication" should get some laughs to start your show.
- You can get a classmate to be the straight person and do a "knock, knock" joke. Or other jokes. Practice until the recording sounds good. Save it. Audiences do not like clip art and images that are unrelated to the main topic, but they tolerate and appreciate irrelevant sounds if they are genuinely funny.
- You and a classmate can sing something short you both know, even an advertising jingle. Then click on Effects then on Increase Speed (by 100%). It will sound like the "Chipmunks Xmas Song."
- Use the Insert, Movie or Sound, Sound from File, menu choices.
- Embed the sound with its effects in an animated graphic.

Summary of 6 ways to add sound to PPT

Here's a **summary** of the six ways to embed sound into Powerpoint®, in the order they appear in the Effect Options dialog box. "Record Narration" and prerecorded sounds are already embedded for you. You must embed the others

The list begins with sounds made using the menu commands Insert, Movies or Sounds, **RECORD SOUND.** Their order is chronological, with most recent on top.

Precorded sounds which come with Powerpoint® appear next. They are alphabetized.

Downloaded sounds- scroll to the last choice, **"Other Sounds…"** A browsing or navigation window opens. Find the sound file and insert it.

Sounds created using **Windows Sound Recorder program**. Scroll to the last choice, **Other Sounds…** and again, show Powerpoint® where the sound is.

Sounds created using the menu commands **Insert, Movies or Sounds, SOUND FROM FILE…** Scroll to the last choice, **Other Sounds…** and again, show Powerpoint® where the sound is.

If we do NOT embed it, then the sound must be in the same folder as the show when we record it and when we present it.

Sounds created using **Slide Show, Record Narration**... are always reliable. Prerecorded sounds are also embedded but there are very few to pick from. Embed the other 4 types.

To turn the volume up within Windows®:

Remember that narration (covered earlier) squelches other kinds of sound on the same slide.

First, here are 3 ways to preview sounds in editing mode.
- Double-click an icon to preview sounds in editing view.
- Click the "play" button in the custom animation task pane.
- Use Shift + F5 to start Slide Show mode at that slide.

Locate the icon of a speaker in the bottom right corner of the monitor screen or desktop, close to the time display (the System Tray.)
- Click it once.
- If "mute" is checked click to remove the checkmark.
- Set the volume higher and listen again for sound.
- If no sound or weak sound is still a problem, this time double click the sound control (System Tray speaker icon).
- This brings up the Windows Volume Control® settings with extensive controls and options.
- Remove the Mute check on "Wave Control" and maximize its output . If there is no check mark beside "Select" click to add one.

Listen for your sound again. Can you hear sound playing? If not, read the panels below, which deal with setting properties in the Recording Control dialog box.

Turn the Windows® microphone on.

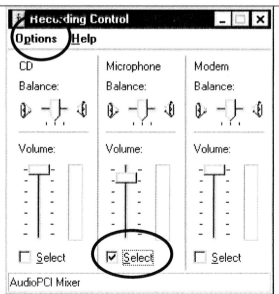

Recording: Microphone is **on**; Playback: Microphone is **off**.

Double click the sound icon (loudspeaker) on the System Tray (the lower right of the screen).

Remove the mute checkmark from both Wave Balance and Volume Control and raise the volume.

Make wave balance & microphone both look like Microphone Balance on the left.

A second way is click on Start, Programs, Accessories, Multimedia, Volume Control.

Click the menu choice OPTIONS. then click on PROPERTIES.

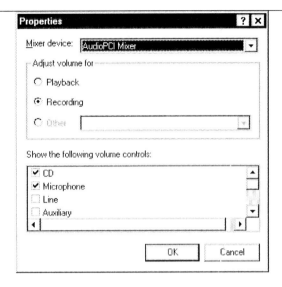

The dialog box on the left appears. The next steps turn the microphone on during recording and off during playback.

Click the radio button next to Recording.

Also put a check mark next to microphone.

Click the OK button. The previous Recording Control dialog box reappears.

The steps above apply to Recording Controls, not Playback.

Note that the check box below the volume control again either gives you the choice "Select" or else it says "Mute." If Mute is checked (on), then remove it. If Select is checked (on) leave it on. If Select is not checked, select it with a check mark. Hit the OK button.

Turn the microphone off in playback

These steps prevent an annoying **feedback screech**.

CLICK Options, Properties, Playback, and remove the selected check mark next to microphone.

REMOVE any check mark next to microphone – that's how you get the screeching, humming feedback, by having the microphone on during playback instead of recording.

Click the OK button.

Photos & the old Picture Toolbar

The buttons we used most functioned to raise brightness, lower brightness, and crop a picture. These buttons were on the Picture Tool Bar in 2003. Selecting any graphic activated that toolbar. Today clicking a picture activates Picture Tools then Format activates choices for editing graphics.

CROP

Select a picture that you have pasted on a slide.

The words PICTURE TOOLS immediately appear on the Quack Title Bar.

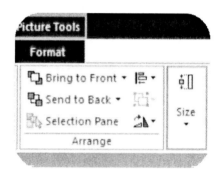

We immediately click beneath it on the Quack Menu command **FORMAT**.

Four Ribbon tab headings appear: ADJUST then PICTURE STYLES and ARRANGE and a large Button for SIZE which has a list box arrow beside it. The figure shows the last two.

Click the **SIZE** button. We could type in its new dimensions if we knew what to fill in. More likely we would CROP an image. Select the **CROP** tool.

The mouse cursor becomes a "T" shaped figure when we pass it over one of the eight CROP HANDLES that appear on graphics when they are selected.

The square handles serve a different function than the circular handles.

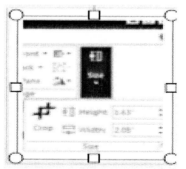

Four handles are squares; they are ideal for cropping one side at a time.

The four circles in the corners are for resizing a picture not for cropping. Corner resizing handles let us enlarge or shrink a graphic without distorting it.

Crop before resizing. Only the best part of a graphic should be enlarged for zooming in on features

deselect the crop tool

When you finish cropping, click the crop button again to cancel or deselect it. If you forget to deselect the tool, here's what happens. If you drag any **corner** of a selected graphic object, it normally either expands or shrinks the graphic. If the picture still has cropping handles dragging a corner to resize the picture does not make it larger, it uncrops the picture instead.

The menu often reverts to HOME. If so, click FORMAT, SIZE, CROP.

UNDEREXPOSED

Most .PPT shows display dark, dingy photos. Does everyone take under-exposed photos? No. This under-exposed photo makes the presenter look like a dufus. Making data look good in turn makes us look good.

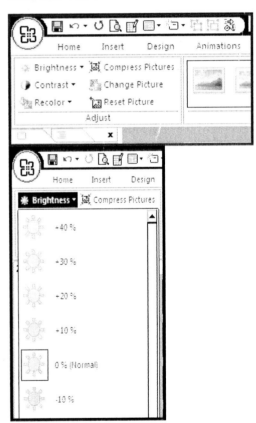

To reach the new brightness controls SELECT a photograph. The words PICTURE TOOLS pops onto the right edge of the Quack Title Bar.

Under that choice is FORMAT. Click on FORMAT.

The first tab heading says ADJUST.

Click the arrow head beside BRIGHTNESS on the ADJUST Tab Heading

COUNT how far you deviate from zero. But where do you look to judge when you reach "it." And where is "it?"

Each time you brighten the photo more details will be revealed. In the Panda photo the right front leg appears in the left foreground. Details appear in the rocks behind the Panda.

When another 10% change in brightness reveals no new details the picture is almost optimized. ALMOST!

OPTIMIZING PHOTO BRIGHTNESS

We just optimized the photo for a hypothetical slide show using the monitor of a portable computer without a slide projector attached. That can be done in a small, intimate conference room. In a large room we must use a projector to be fair to people in the back of that room.

The photo optimized for monitor output will always appear 25% darker when it bounces off the white screen. That white cloth surface is not a mirror so it does not reflect 99% of incoming light as a mirror would. The white cloth absorbs about 25 to 30 percent reflecting only 75% of the incoming light. It will look 25% darker. That's why we should click the brightness button some more after we reach the "no new details" stage. When it looks a little too bright on the monitor it will look just right on the screen.

Pictures viewed on a monitor seem underexposed (left). We used the increase brightness button (right picture).

Start a photo looking like the one on the right to end up looking like the left one.

The projected image bounces off a screen that absorbs light.

Where to look

to optimize photos of people? Look at the bridge of the nose between the eyebrows. A second location is the bottom of the nose where it attaches to the face. When you can't see improvement of details there, the photo is optimized for the monitor. Two to three further brightness clicks maximizes it for slide show presentation. This has to be tested to be believed.

deselect the crop tool

When you finish cropping, click the crop button again to cancel or deselect it. If you forget to deselect the tool, here's what happens. If you drag any **corner** of a selected graphic object, it normally either expands or shrinks the graphic. If the picture has cropping handles dragging a corner to resize the picture does not make it larger, it un-crops the picture instead.

screen prints

A screen print is an exact copy of the whole computer monitor screen at some instant. Suppose you visit a web site that plays a video clip related to your topic. You can make a screen print of an appropriate scene then insert it as a picture on your slide. You have to trim the unrelated parts of the screen using the crop tool on the Picture Toolbar.

A text button or a graphic button can be hyperlinked to a web site if you find one with a relevant video clip you want to show. Make a screen print of into a linked button.

If you hyperlink a graphic you **can't** also animate the same object or the link won't work. Screen prints are valuable for teaching people how to do software tasks. Take a snapshot of each changed screen and make them into individual slides.

Insert a screen print

Find the Print Screen button at the top right of the keyboard, just to the right of F12, Function 12 key. When you push it, a copy of the monitor screen is placed on the office clipboard. The button should actually be named copy screen not print screen.

Switch over to the slide show and paste the image. Use the crop tool on the picture toolbar to trim irrelevant parts of the image. Deselect the tool before resizing the picture. Use one of the four corner resizing handles to make the picture larger or smaller without distorting it.

color button disappeared into Picture Styles

The second button from the left was the color button. The choices on it are automatic color (the original picture), grayscale, black and white and washout (formerly watermark). These have been expanded nicely into the Picture Styles ribbon tab heading. Select a picture then click FORMAT, PICTURE STYLES. The above screen print ought to make you eager to investigate this more.

Grayscale can make an image look older in a few cases. It can decrease the size of the graphic in memory. It can show you how it will print on a non-color printer.

The choice **black and white** has no gray. Not all pictures look neat in pure black and white, but the ones that do are worth the time. It makes a photo look like a painting.

photographs & effectiveness

An excellent rule of writing is, "**Don't tell me, show me.**" Don't tell the reader a person said something, quote those words exactly and let the reader decide what the speaker meant. In PPT, don't just describe a conflict or an object, show photographs of them. Authoring slide shows is not so different from authoring essays or short stories, except books can't use sounds and video clips.

Photographs, screen prints, animated cartoon drawn figures and even clip art should appear on nearly every slide. The more you use **relevant graphics** the more the audience will like your show.

Try using **Google's Image Search**. Type in a key word or phrase. Odds are it will retrieve more good hits than you look at in your lifetime, many relevant to your topic.

People complain about **boredom** at slide shows; no surprise if their brains were riddled by bullets (text). Colored text is still text.

Instantly zoom in and out

If all we display are words, why not just show the audience a MS Word® document? You can zoom in or out to make your plain document fill the screen with the following keyboard shortcut.

Hold the **Control Key** down with one hand and move the **mouse wheel** forward or backward. The shortcut works in many other MS applications. Why not just hand the audience the hard copies and ask if they have any questions? A slide show has to beat that or it's just a waste of time.

Do photos cure boredom?

Photos interrupt boredom but interaction with the audience eliminates its source.

Every few slides, ask a question and shut up until some audience members try to answer your question. Coax them. Discuss it with them. Then continue the monologue briefly until the next question. Make them reflect on what they just saw. Example: "Which approach recently would you use, and why?"

Order of appearance

There are three basic objects on slides. In order of appearance, the slide should start with appearance of a title placeholder, 1 or more graphic objects, then bulleted or paragraph style text animated to arrive last.

As we talk, audience members are forming pictures in their minds. If we talk about flying prey, we should present a photo of a butterfly. It relieves the audience of forming the image of an example and it speeds comprehension. Display the graphic image before the text. Graphics provide a **scaffold** on which to hang new knowledge.

title, picture, text

The title placeholder is an advance organizer. Some people don't see the need for a title on every slide, but it is essential for both the designer and the audience.

Objects not animated appear first. Therefore, always put a descriptive title on every slide but never animate a title place holder. Pick a couple of keywords; make them a title.

The second feature should be your graphic images. They can be un-animated so they already are on the slide when the slide and its title appear. Graphic images can also be animated to appear before the bulleted text. Change the graphic's position on slides for variety.

While you're animating a graphic, you can embed sounds into the animated graphic using the Effect Options dialog box in custom animation's task pane.

Use "Callouts" on the menu Draw, Autoshapes, to make graphic people and animals talk to the audience, comic book style. Use Comic Sans MS Font.

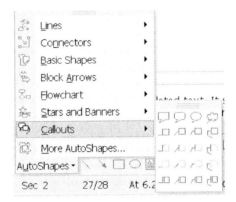

Click the Drawing toolbar: Autoshapes, Callouts, &

Silence the bullets!

Last to appear is bulleted text. Animating bullets cures cluttered screens, distractions, and memory overload. Have the bulleted text box come on one bullet at a time, after the graphics. Never add sound to bulleted text. The sound will repeat on each bullet and annoy the audience.

Order of Appearance - Review

1. The **title** appears first because it is not animated at all.
2. **Photos**, clip art, animated GIFs appear next.
   a. They can be unanimated like the Title is.
   b. If animated, the speed should be very fast or fast.
3. Any **bulleted text** arrives last.
   a. Bulleted text should usually be custom animated
   b. Fast or Very Fast
   c. From the Basic List.
   d. Must not move across the screen but be revealed in its final place, in some pattern like circle or blinds or dissolve.
   e. Fly In, Crawl In, Random Effects all turn an audience off.

Graphics

The original image left will be reflected off the projector screen, not seen straight through the monitor. The white cloth projector screen will absorb perhaps 30% of the light. It will appear 30% darker. Most details will be hidden.

It has a Title placeholder with Arial Black font. The text box below has Comic Sans MS.

Notice the textbox is lighter than the rest of the photograph, but not opaque white.

Pure white would block out the image. **Transparent fill color** was used in addition to a white fill color. This example is 80% transparent inside the text box. Only 1 in 5 pixels has white color.

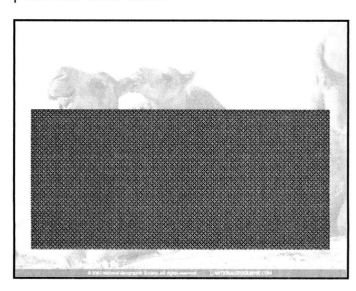

The same photo was brightened using the button on the Picture Toolbar. See all the detail missing previously was restored (below).

It's OK, they're married camels!

This picture comes from the **wildly** popular web site www. NationalGeographic.com from their "Picture of the Day" archive.

We suggest when you browse the previous year's collection of pictures of the day, be certain to budget a lot of time. Many of the photographs are so interesting- you are compelled to stop and reflect.

We have all seen amateurs try to force text onto slide backgrounds that are impossible to decipher. Even national magazines will go crazy and try to force text onto a photographed background when there is no contrast between text and background. It is strange no one ever writes in to say they can't read the words. If all you concentrate on is simple legibility, you'll turn out better quality work than 90% of the print media.

Using relevant photographs, make your own beautiful template backgrounds. They will be prettier, more relevant, and easier to read text from, than the ones Microsoft® paid graphic artists to develop. The only difficult part is choosing one, because you have to reflect on many before you spot one that is worth the wait.

Suppose our talk is about dehydration and we want to use this unusual camel photo. Just because we want to use it does not alone make it suitable.

We need to click the menu choices **Insert, Picture**, and point to it. In Powerpoint© 2007 Insert, Picture means Picture from file not clip art.

The Draw Menu Became

Format Menu, ARRANGE Tab Heading

Once the picture is inserted on the Slide and enlarged to cover the slide completely we have to solve a problem. The photograph is on top of the title placeholder and the bulleted text box. We can't enter text on any such slides.

On the Home menu the ribbon has tab headings for DRAWING.

We click the large toolbar button ARRANGE.

From its drop down list box we choose SEND TO BACK. See the screen print on the next page for details.

Now the textboxes are on top of the photo not covered up.

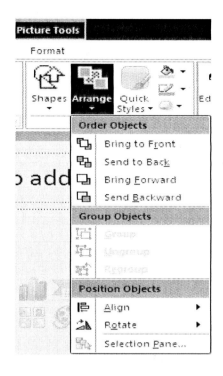

The **ARRANGE** tab heading on the HOME menu is handy. Before half its choices will work it is necessary to select or click on a graphic first.

Notice we can use the ARRANGE button to ORDER multiple layers, to GROUP objects, to ALIGN and to ROTATE.

We would change the font face for the title placeholder to Arial Black because it throws a lot of ink on the slide but also has wide spacing between letters.

We change the bulleted text box to Comic Sans MS because it has wide kerning (left to right spacing which makes it easy to read).

Please look at the earlier photograph, the one with font names. It will not be hard to read slide titles with that as a template because the light blue sky across the top makes a black title font a natural title choice. It will be harder to read bulleted text there as the camel body hair is beige not white. The next technique was designed by MS to solve such problems.

Partially Transparent Fill Color for Photos

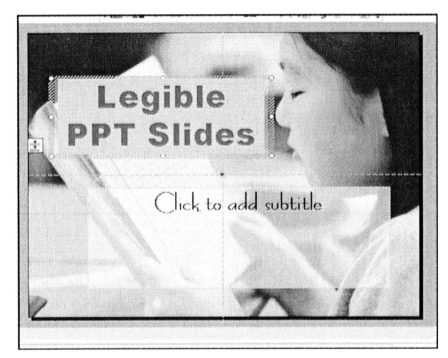

In the previous screen print left: because the enlarged photo covers up the two textboxes, we clicked FORMAT, ARRANGE then SEND TO BACK. That put text placeholders back in front of the photo.

The top textbox shows a descriptive title but the fill color in the title shape hides the picture behind it. Can we see the book's page behind the title? No. We could fix that problem by making the textbox fill color 70-90% partly transparent.

The smaller textbox in the photo above was given a fill color of white. At first, it obliterated the part of the photograph where the hands are holding the book. We experimented by trial and error adjusting the % transparency slider bar. You can read the words "Click to add subtitle." You can see the lines of text behind the textbox.

Many PPT authors do not use a fill color at all. Their pictures remain visible but their text is unreadable. You can have both legible text and high clarity of the full photograph with 70% - 90% transparent fill color.

Note: fill color is the color inside a text box and is not the same as slide background color. Always choose color by whether it is very dark or very light, not for fashion reasons. The darkness of text color has to contrast extremely with fill color.

to be legible

If the text is hard to read make the percent transparency less. If the text is easy to read but the photo behind it is not visible, make the percent transparency greater.

Transparent fill color PPT© 2007

We could give the bulleted list box on the left a white fill color. But the opaque white box takes up most of the photograph and completely obscures the camels' bodies.

Right click the border line of the bulleted text box.

Click the last choice **FORMAT SHAPE** and a dialog box opens. See the following screen print for how to make it 80% transparent.

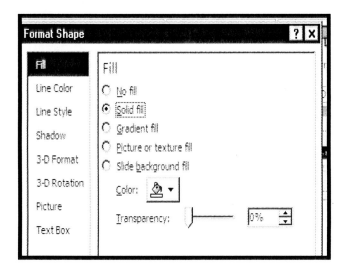

To give the placeholder a partially transparent fill color we choose FILL at the left side of the Format Shape dialog box then SOLID FILL on the right side.

Choose the COLOR to be WHITE then note the TRANSPARENCY SLIDER at the bottom.

We will find the optimum setting between 70% and 90% by trial-and-error.

DRAG the dialog box to one side so you can see the textbox as you change settings.

Start the slider bar at **70% transparent**. The text will usually be quite legible but there will be too much white in the textbox.

Stop to reflect. We found a lovely picture but the textbox white fill color is like someone imposed a huge billboard blocking the view.

It needs to less white; more transparent.

The more we slide the transparency box to the right, the better the picture. Compare the fireplace details here at 90% to the earlier version at 70%.

The more we click the slider box to the left, (previous picture) the better we can see the words.

What we get in exchange for patience going back and forth with this slide bar, is an unusual slide background that is prettier and easier to read text off of, than templates supplied by Microsoft.

Rotate or Flip

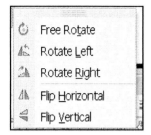

↻	Free Rotate
⬑	Rotate Left
⬏	Rotate Right
⬎	Flip Horizontal
⬐	Flip Vertical

Sometimes you scan a page at right angles to the intended direction or even upside down. Once it's in PPT, you can click on DRAW, Rotate or Flip and fix the alignment problem without having to scan the image again.

Use the Flip Horizontal command to change the apparent direction of a car or animal. If a horse is galloping left or a shark is swimming left, but the rest of the action is off to the right, flip your picture horizontally and the action will make sense. Also, if you draw an arrow pointing the wrong way, use the rotate or flip command to flip it horizontally or vertically.

Align or Distribute

For Group, or for Align or Distribute to be active at least two objects must be selected.

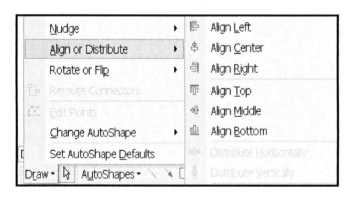

Nudge ▶	▣ Align Left
Align or Distribute ▶	♣ Align Center
Rotate or Flip ▶	▣ Align Right
Reroute Connectors	▥ Align Top
Edit Points	▥ Align Middle
Change AutoShape ▶	▥ Align Bottom
Set AutoShape Defaults	▥ Distribute Horizontally
Draw ▾ ▷ AutoShapes ▾ ＼ ＼ ▢	▥ Distribute Vertically

To align two objects by their top borders choose Align Top and so forth.

To select multiple objects hold the SHIFT key down while clicking each object. Shift-click toggles both on and off.

Order Layers

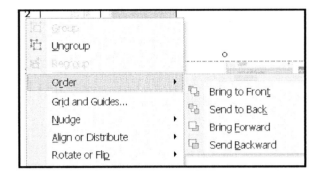

To change which transparent layer loads first, etc.:

click on DRAW, ORDER,
a) then Bring to the Front
b) or Back,
c) Bring Forward one layer,
d) or Backward one layer.

Each object placed on a slide goes into a unique invisible layer.

Nudge, Arrow Keys

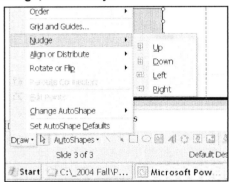

Nudge lets you move an object **less distance** than the mouse can.

The same motion is gotten by tapping the arrow navigation key once.

Arrow keys are at the bottom right of the keyboard.

Grid & Guides

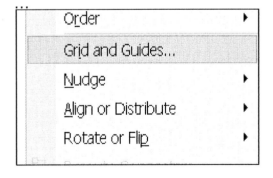

Grid & Guides choices are on both the View Menu and DRAW menu. If we turn them on they mark the exact center of our slides in editing view.; great for balancing slide elements.

They disappear in Slide Show Mode.

They can be dragged into different spots. Most authors leave them on all the time.

The Grid & Guides Dialog Box

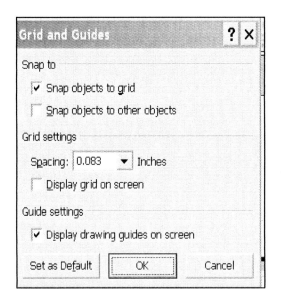

When you select Grid and Guides the top choice is "Snap to Grid."

Objects seem to snap onto invisible gridlines without guidance from your hand. This saves your shoulder and wrist.

When you select an object and tap the arrow navigation keys once, it moves 1/12 of an inch. You can't do that with your mouse.

Snap to grid

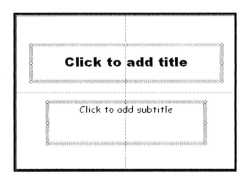

Showing the guidelines makes sense; showing the **gridlines** makes the slide look like a piece of graph paper.

If you choose "Snap to grid" then the nearest grid line is the closest one can approach an object.

So when an arrow won't line up, take the check mark away from "Snap to grid" and try again.

Shift-Click & Group, Ungroup

Suppose you have to assemble a drawing using multiple drawing tools. To keep everything together, select several objects and choose Group from the top of the DRAW menu.

To select several objects hold the Shift key down with one hand and click those objects one at a time. Then choose DRAW, Group. It toggles on and off.

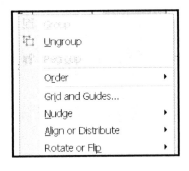

After Grouping several items they seem to behave as one. They move as one, stretch and shrink as one object. But you can't edit them separately unless you Ungroup them.

Assignment 2 – Guess "Who Am I?"

Make an 8-slide show about a famous person, deceased, who is in history books. Bring out details about why they are famous including their achievements, philosophy, or accomplishments. Gradually uncover a little more about them on every slide. Do not name the mystery figure in the title or on slide 1. Give their identity on the last slide.

Directions: Submit a slide show that teases your audience with hints on slides 2-7 but reveals the historical mystery person on the last slide. **Each slide** has 2 to 4 bullets and a RELEVANT graphic image. The bullets appear one at a time, are 28 point font, and are very legible. **Each slide** has background fill effects as described in detail below. Remember the various fill effects should be designed so the background is either light or dark but not streaked with light and dark both in the background.

Applies to:	Directions
Master Slide	Replace Arial in both placeholders with a better font face.
Slide 1 Title	Who Am I? then your name and class time
Format, Background:	
Slide 1 Title	Fill Effects, two colors gradient tab
Slide 2	Fill Effects, one color shaded on gradient tab
3	Fill Effects, PRESET colors gradient tab
4	Fill Effects, two colors gradient tab
5	Fill Effects, one solid color background
6	Fill Effects, choose one from the TEXTURE tab
7	Photo background, transparent fill color in textboxes
8	Different Photo background, transp. fill color in textboxes
8	Identify the famous person. Must be someone included in history textbooks because of their accomplishments.
title placeholders	**DO NOT animate title boxes!**
Graphics	
Photographs	IF animated only use VERY FAST speed From any category
One photo plus 2 to 4 bullets on 7 of the 8 slides	
Bulleted text	Follows graphics in sequence on each slide.
	Choose text effects listed under "BASIC"
	But NOT crawl in, fly in, or random effects
	Speed either very fast or fast- no others
	Each bullet appears separately not all the bullets at once
	Very Fast or Fast speed for animations not Medium.
Transparent Fill Color	One slide (your pick) has an enlarged photo for its background and uses transparent fill color of 70%-90% in textboxes.
Text must be Very Dark if Background is Very Light	And if B/G is very dark then the text is very light.

Assignment 3: Spy Voices

Value	90 pts (9 slides minimum at 10 pts each)
Story Line	

		Tell about your one greatest adventure as a master spy. Spies steal information not money or diamonds. Spies steal information, assassins murder. This is a spy story that **depends on an overheard conversation.** Make the recording of your voice doing both parties or get a friend to be one voice. Examples: broke the Orange Code of N. Korea; stole the formula for blue M&M candies; copied the secret Swiss bank account numbers of the Enron upper management. One student wrote about needing to steal the recipe for a famous barbeque sauce because his countrymen in Cambodia raised much beef successfully but without a good sauce they were emigrating to Texas. Cambodia sent him to steal the recipe.
Master Slide		Replace Title font with Arial Black and bulleted textbox with one chosen from the following: Comic Sans MS, Papyrus, Stylus BT, or Kidprint. Animate the bulleted list box following the rules for effective animation. Return to Normal View.
Features:		
Every Slide		**One photo on each slide; appears before textboxes do.**
Every Slide		**Has two to four bulleted text items**; individually custom animated to appear singly without moving around.
Title slide		**Music**: Insert, Media Clips, Sound from Clip Gallery. Find a suspenseful music clip for the country the tale takes place in. **Once it starts it plays for TWO slides so the second slide has no other sounds**
Slide 2 - a Concept Map with two total links; both targets return to the Map		Use photos/ screen prints of the characters, or text about the plot – 4 to 7 Map objects, 2 are linked. There are examples all over this text.
One Slide of your choice		**An overheard embedded sound** – a 2-person conversation that plays with the animated photo.
One Slide of your choice		**A photo linked to a web site** which then plays any action scene like a video of a chase, fight, something suspenseful. State in the textbox what to do when the reader reaches that site. This photo will not be animated just linked. Use Mozilla Firefox if you have it available as a browser.
One Slide of your choice		**Sound Effect: an animal guarding the secrets (a mean duck, hungry wolf, killer woodpecker)**
One Slide of your choice		**Sound Effect: a storm with thunder and wind**
(A great source of sound effects is Findsounds.com – right click and pick Save Target As or Save Link As)		ALL Sounds must be embedded in a graphic that is custom animated; however, the one link to a web video is not animated.

Last slide:	Your recorded voice. Comment, wrap up, moralize – say what you think a TV station would say at end of adventure hour or story hour.
Minimum slides	At least 9 slides. More are welcome.
DO NOT USE	Slide Show, Record Narration.

Grading Rubric: Spy Voices.ppt

Value	90 pts	
Due midnight Tuesday	March 6, 2007	
Story Line 10	Tell about your one greatest achievement as a master spy.	
Master Slide 10	Replace Arial in both textboxes with a more legible font face. Format background for highest legibility and best color contrast between text and background.	
Return to Normal View.		
Features: 10	One photo on each slide; appears before textboxes	
10	Two to four bulleted text items; individually custom animated to appear singly without moving around.	
Title slide 5-10-15	Music: Insert, Media, Sound from Clip Gallery. Title also identifies student & class section.	
Slide 2 - a Concept Map (15) with two total links; both targets return to the Map	Use RELEVANT photos or screen prints of the characters, or text about the plot – 4 to 7 objects, 2 are linked.	
One Slide of your choice 10	An overheard embedded sound – a conversation that plays when the animated photo appears.	
One Slide of your choice 10	A photo linked to a web site which then plays some action scene like a video of a chase, fight, something suspenseful. State in the textbox what to do when the reader reaches that site. This photo will not be animated just linked. Use Firefox if you have it available as a browser.	
One Slide of your choice 10	Sound Effect: an animal guarding the secrets	
One Slide of your choice 10	Sound Effect: a storm with thunder and wind	
	ALL Sounds must be embedded in a graphic that is custom animated. The link to a video is not animated.	
Last slide: 10	Your recorded voice. Comment, wrap up, moralize – say what you think a TV station would say at end.	
Minimum slides 10	At least 9 slides. More are welcome. +10 possible.	
DO NOT USE	Slide Show, Record Narration	
Embed sounds/music within animated graphics. Check the photos for Effect Options for embedded sounds. Embedded sounds play without double clicking an icon.		

Assignment 4: Stamped Envelope

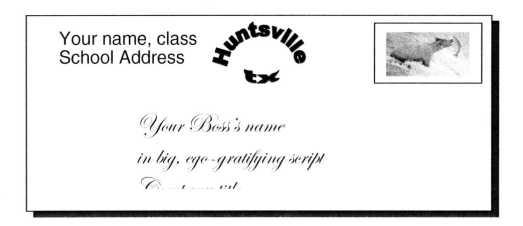

The following exercise uses several tools on the old DRAWING toolbar.

Goal: The output will look like a mock envelope with a stamp, postmark, and both return address and delivery address. True purpose: kiss up to the boss by presenting their name in large letters. Find a photograph of the boss's hobby not your own. Make it into a stamp with a price on it. Postmark the envelope using Word Art.

Drag a rectangle using the rectangle tool on the DRAWING toolbar. It is by default, filled with a hideous shade of seasick blue. Double click the rectangle border. Choose a white fill color from the top of the dialog box. Your stomach already feels better.

Duplicate that white rectangle (envelope). Select the rectangle; use Control + D. Double click this second rectangle's border to turn it into a **black (fill) shadow** for a 3-D effect on the envelope. Hit OK.

Hold the SHIFT key down while you left click once on each of the two rectangles, black and white. This allows both to be selected at once. Go to the DRAW menu, the top choice: **Group.** Now they will not move apart while you put other elements on the envelope.

Locate the Text Tool, the one to our left. The Tool Tip says Text Tool. Click it. Drag a shape left to right to show it where you want the line to break. Type your name.

Hold down the SHIFT key while you strike the Enter key. Shift + Enter is known as a **soft return.**

A hard return adds paragraph formatting to the Enter Key, but a soft return does not. When you need to conserve vertical space in a column use soft returns.

Select the Text Tool again and drag a shape to show it where the lines will break when we put in the **deliver to** address (the boss's). Use soft returns to conserve vertical space (Shift + Enter = soft return). Type in your boss's address.

Select the rectangle tool and hold the shift key down while you draw with it in the upper right corner of the envelope. This produces a symmetrical square not a rectangle. This will serve as your stamp.

Inside the stamp boundary will go a price $0.32 and a picture or clip art. What to choose for the picture? What is the boss's hobby? Putting a picture of **your own** personal hobby is not going to advance your career. Ask, what does the boss enjoy or talk about often? Use Insert, Picture, Clip Art, then type in that phrase in the search field.

Next make an imitation postmark using Word Art.

	Click the Word Art button on the left here. An editing box opens that lets us choose the geometric shape of the words. Pick the top half of an arch for the city and later the bottom of the arch for state. Choose Arial Black font NOT Times New Roman. Make the font size 12 points. Type in your city for the top bending arch. Go through the Word Art process again and choose the bottom bending arch. Match the font size and type. Type in the name of the state.

Save the .PPT file as "Envelope.PPT." and print it. Pass the mouse pointer over the remaining buttons on the DRAW tool bar. Learn how to use them one at a time. When you animate any arrows use "Wipe." If the arrow points downward Wipe Down effect makes it look like some invisible hand is drawing the arrow right there on screen.

Link to video clips on the web

Our show would be more enjoyable if it included say 30 seconds' worth of video. Including video clips in MS PowerPoint© is easy. The only part that takes time is searching for a good video clip. We don't need to postpone it until we are more skilled. We don't have to first learn all the file extensions for all video types.

Let's look at the choices we have to make. The first one is "How can we find a video clip without spending enormous blocks of time?"

First do a search using Google's Advanced Search, then we'll link a picture or clip art to that web site. Clicking the link will start a web browser that goes to the video site. When we've seen enough of the video clip we close the browser window and automatically return to the show in slide show view.

There are two steps to review: finding a good video clip, and linking to the web site (or other ways). Use the **Google Advanced Search**. Continuing clockwise below, if we fail to find one we can make our own video clip. If we find one on the web we hyperlink to the web page. If we make our own video clip we use the Insert menu choice but there are a couple of points to remember so it will play reliably (later).

First go to the home page of Google.com, not the mini-search bar. Complete the four circled areas shown below.

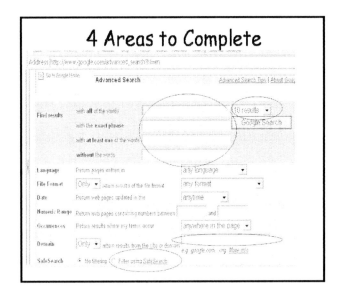

Whenever we search for "Video" we turn on "Filter using Safe Search" to block pornographic web sites. We also include "Without the words" to read "Games" so we don't get a large number of useless hits about video games. Other words to put in the "Without the Words" field include "$ Buy Sale Cassette Cassettes." This cuts down the advertising from commercial sites.

It is a good idea to change the "Number of results" at the very top to 100 instead of 10. We'll do a much finer search If the 200th hit was truly useless it would not have appeared in the list in the first place. We can't judge solely by the name of the web site. A completed example follows:

2-Word Exact Phrase Is Best

The best searches involve two-word searches in the field named "Exact Phrase." When a student tried "Roman Empire" in the exact phrase field, there were no longer any unwanted hits for Roman Sculpture or Roman Numbers, or the Ottoman Empire. Only Roman Empire hits showed up.

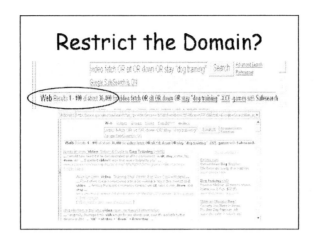

Restrict the Domain?

Here's another handy tip from students. Before examining any hits read the top blue and white banner before we scroll down. This result gave the student 36,400 web sites. We can restrict the top-level domain to one of three domains that don't have so much advertising to eliminate (.edu, .gov, .org)

Change the "Domain" field to read "Only return results from the site or domain _____." We can only restrict this to one domain at a time. First type in ".edu."

If the first 300 hits are not relevant go back and change the Domain field to ".org" which brings up mostly non-profit organizations. If ".edu" and ".org" aren't good enough, substitute ".gov" and you might find a wealth of treasure.

If those don't work, go to the web sites for NationalGeographic.com or PBS.com. - both are gold mines for beautiful photographs, fascinating facts and quality reporting. Or, you might try any of the large news sites like ABC or CBS news, or Getty.org, all of which have extensive film libraries.

If those sites don't work try changing the top field from "video" to "Video archive." Then try different key words until you find a good video.

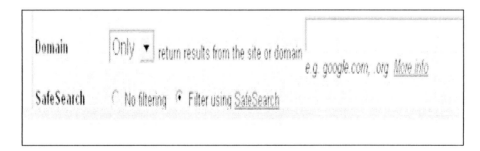

Linking a photo to a video on the web-

We can place either some text to make hypertext, or a graphic image to make a hypermedia link on a PowerPoint© slide. This will link that web site with the video to our presentation. The best choices are a graphic object like a photograph, an animated GIF, or clip art. Much clip art is awful. Linking text is less interesting.

Copying and Pasting a Relevant Image -

The best still images we've found on the web were discovered with Google. This time, instead of clicking on Advanced Search, click at the very top of the Google home page where it says "Images." Type in selected keywords related to your topic.

In Internet Explorer on Google Images, when you see good results right-click them and pick "Save Picture As." In Netscape the choice says "Save Image As." Start at the top of the Save As dialog box. At the very top type in the location where to save it. Choose to save it in the same folder you have your slide show in. Give it an intelligent file name, one that describes the contents of the picture.

Place the Image on a slide -

In PowerPoint© place the image on a slide using "Insert, Picture, From File." Point to the graphic you saved to use as a link. Insert it.

Copy the web site's URL to the Office Clipboard -

Using the web browser again go to the web site that your excellent video clip plays on. Click the URL, or also called the address box, or a locator box. Copy the web address to the Office Clipboard using the keyboard shortcut Control + C.

Create the link from the picture to the web site for the video.

Click once on that picture to select it. With the photograph selected, click the menu choices "Slide Show, Action Settings, Hyperlink to, and then scroll. Scroll down to "URL…"

In the dialog box Paste the URL (the address) using the keyboard shortcut "Control + V" (paste). Hit two OK buttons and you are linked. You have to place the presentation in View, Slide Show to see it work.

Before presenting, load your slide slow onto the computer connected to the projector. Put it in slide show, test the volume, and start the web browser. Go to the web site with the video clip. Minimize the browser. Now when we click the photo link to the web site, there will only be a short delay before the video starts.

If the video is too long, you don't have to play the whole thing. Whenever you close the browser window, you return to the slide show in Slide Show View.

Now for the case where a video clip is vital to the success of the slide show, but there isn't one on the web.

Suppose you make your own video clip as an **Apple Quick Time Movie©**. PowerPoint© is made by Microsoft© which doesn't want to cooperate with this format.

Normally, you would make a video clip, import it into video editing software, then save it as a compressed digital file. You would locate it in the same folder as your slide show file when you pasted it and keep it in the same folder when you play it.

IF your video clip is a type that Windows supports, not Apple Quick Time© all you have to do is click the menu choices "Insert, Movie or Sound, Movie from File." Use the browser window to locate it.

Don't use the menu choices "Insert, Movie or Sound, Movie from file…" if you created an Apple Quick Time© video clip. **There is an easy, reliable way to play it.** First make sure you've downloaded a free Apple Quick Time Player© to the computer that will play the Quick Time© video clip. Then skip over the Insert menu choice. Click the menu choices Slide Show, Action Buttons (not action settings, action buttons). Choose the button of a video camcorder in the lower right corner.

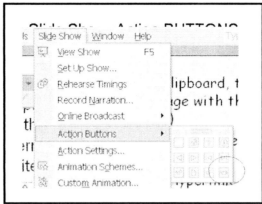

Your pointer becomes a crosshair not an arrow.

Draw a rectangular shape using the camcorder button tool. You can resize it later. Later you can double click it to change the color of the button. When you draw the shape, the hyperlink dialog box appears. Choose the radio button that says "**Run Program...**". A "**Select Program to Run**" dialog box appears. Point to and click on the file in the dialog box window. Hit OK buttons twice to complete it.

Put the slide show in Slide Show View and click the camcorder button.

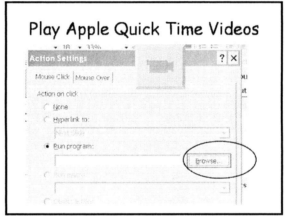

Use the Text tool on the Draw Tool Bar

to make text boxes. Find it three lines above the bottom of the monitor. Place your cursor on the eighth button from the left which is a letter "A" with stripes beside it. Click it for a half-second and release it. If it stays selected when you release it, your cursor takes the shape of an I-beam or sword.

The text tool on the "Draw" tool bar. Novices think you have to stretch exactly the right shape on the slide before typing with the text tool. Untrue.

You only have to approximately show Powerpoint® how wide the line is supposed to be. All you show it is where the line break occurs. If you err, just stretch the resizing handle on one side after you make the text box. There is no need to be slow & careful, just stretch any old width and move on.

117

Format the First Concept Map Textbox

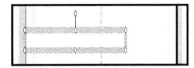

Drag an arbitrary shape with the text tool. You can change your mind about its width later

First type "Visible Symptoms" and hit the Escape Key. That selects all the text at once for faster editing. Hold down the Control Key and strike the letter "E" which stands for "Center." Remember you do copy (Control + C) much more often than center, so when it came time for a centering command, the programmers went to the second letter of the word "center".

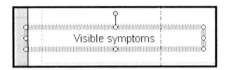

Centered, 28 point font size, selected all. Next is Control + T.

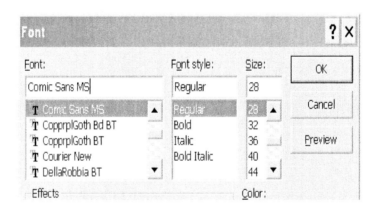

The format font dialog box.

Start typing the font name as soon as the box appears and it scrolls to that part of the list that matches the first 3 letters typed.

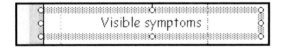

28 point centered Comic Sans MS, checkered border. Format a textbox to look like a control button.

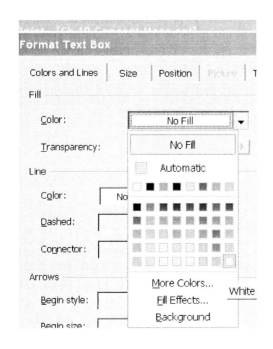

After you double click the border of the text box change "No fill" to a white color for now. Later if you wish you can color code some branches of your concept map. You should use a white font color inside any darkly-filled text box, for better legibility.

It can be an advantage to give text boxes on a concept map a fill color. By using the draw menu commands Order, Bring to the front, we can conceal excessive connecting lines by sending them to a further layer in back. We don't have to draw lines as expertly.

add a line around the box

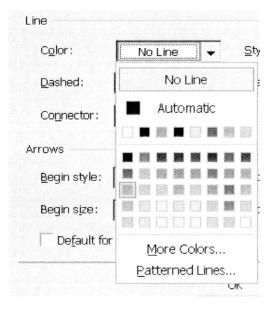

Again double click the text box border, this time to put a colored line around it. That makes it look like a button for hypertext not just plain words on a slide.

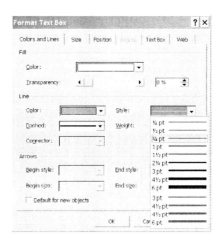

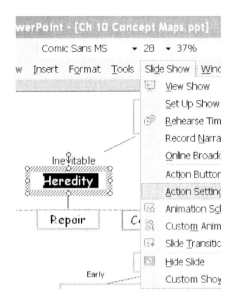

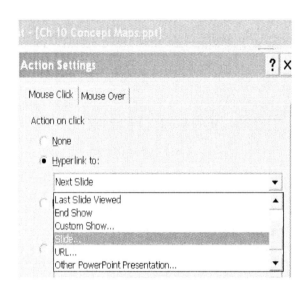

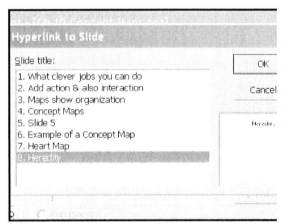

There are two **OK** buttons to accept, one high, one low. If we look at the concept map we see the word heredity underlined but it's in a pale shade of green.

We only have to **change the default colors for hypertext** once in a Powerpoint show and the preference is permanent. **This is one of the best hidden menu choices in all PPT**.

The next problem is the default color is very hard to read. Next we change the default hypertext color into bright, bold colors that show up all over the room. Most presentations that use hyperlinks have links placed on backgrounds that make the links unreadable. There are two colors to change, links and visited links. The color selected is not important, just whether it is a very dark or very light shade.

Changing Hypertext Default Colors

Start by clicking the menu choices **Format, Slide Design...** Look at the right side of the monitor at the Task Pane.

Menu choices:

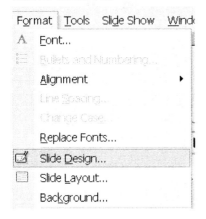

Click on **Color Schemes**.

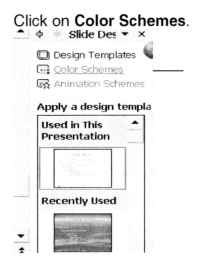

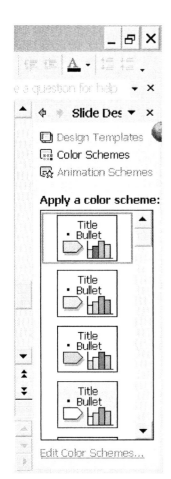

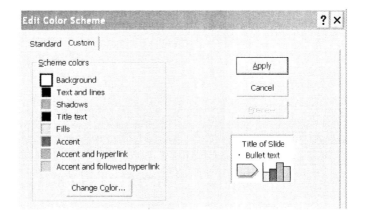

(left figure) UNDERNEATH Click on **Edit Color Schemes...**

On the Custom tab heading, select the next to last colored square for Accent and Hyperlink –unvisited. Click on the "Change Color..." button. A hexagon shaped color palette appears with light colors in the middle and dark on the edge. Click on a **dark blue** color and hit OK.

Click the bottom ("weasel-puke") green color that says "Accent and followed hyperlink." Click the Change Color... button. Choose a very dark color. Hit OK.

Maximize Effectiveness

Most presentations that have ever been given probably wasted the participants' time. You will be pleasantly surprised that about a dozen features built into Powerpoint© increase audience retention by with Instructional Technology strategies.

The Nightly News

Have you ever wondered why every night, the TV weather report can survive without giving you what you want? They waste most your time introducing irrelevant cloud patterns and end by having to race through the 5-day forecast in exactly five seconds. Honestly, if they showed the cloud patterns over Malaysia instead of Texas, would we ever know it? Do you remember the forecast tomorrow better because they spent the extra time to enrich you?

They do this because their *audience analysis* tells them you can't understand cloud patterns but find the segment entertaining. Motion draws the eye. It is your motivation in viewing: to hear/see **tomorrow's forecast**. What is their *purpose?* Is it to bring the weather information to you? Think again. Ask the station manager. Their true purpose is to bring *an audience (that's you) to their advertiser.*

By using multimedia to entertain you, and **presenting too much too fast,** they know you'll return tomorrow and at most, jot down 1 or 2 days' forecasts. And you'll blame your memory but not them for any inability to recall the data. Suppose you grab a pencil and scratch paper right now. Write down everything you can remember from all the news programs you ever watched. Now, would you need a second sheet of paper? Most people would not. All of your life, you've listened to news monologues devoid of audience interaction (no questions asked of you. Was the time spent effectively?

Everyone has a **short-term memory limit** (preceded by a sensory store). People can remember 7 (+/- 2) facts as they acquire data they just heard. After they read about or hear two highs, two lows and 2 rain probabilities, *they have to forget* Monday's forecast to hear Wednesday's data. Our students and colleagues are not different. The nightly news uses these facts to manipulate you into tuning in every night. But you can use these facts to boost effectiveness in your PowerPoint© shows.

Suppose this article was a presentation instead; pretend the speaker has urged you to "Stop after every few slides and ask a question or have them complete an action." If you just presented the five day forecast you could ask "Which day will you most need your umbrella?" This makes an audience rearrange the presented facts to answer. The sensory store which only holds data for a few seconds will move the related facts to short term memory while seriously reflecting on them to rearrange them.

What if you ask a question but they don't answer? Rephrase the question or give hints. Wait longer, because someone in the audience will volunteer an answer eventually. Never answer your own question until the audience has attempted a response.

Replies involve "buy in" to the topic; they might include reciprocal questions. Is the silence awkward? Must you relieve it by answering the question for the audience? No. Is it better to give a hint or to rephrase the question instead? Of course. These meta-questions (How should I word this?) lead to an interaction which improves retention. *Asking a variety of questions can stimulate the listener to rearrange the material in their heads. And learn.*

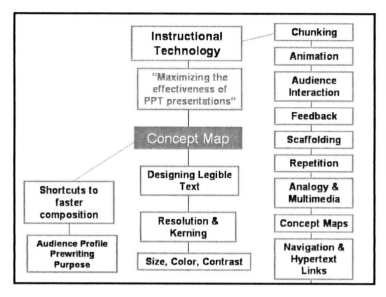

To avoid wasting your time and the audience's time, use audience interaction and the other tools shown on the left.

They come from cognitive psychology research into how to make your points easier to remember.

Note that the use of a concept map is one of the many cognitive tools. If we hyperlink the summarizing map to slides having details we can make learning easier.

Analogy

"Division is like slicing a pizza. It didn't last as long as a rodeo ride does. They listened for a New York minute then interrupted again." *Common life analogies* simplify finding relevant clip art and relevant photos. "Licensing is coming back from decades of decay and inactivity" can be illustrated by searching for "graveyard" images not "licensing." Cognitive psychologists have made the case that **nearly all we learn is through analogy**, by comparison to what is already familiar and known.

Spaced Repetition

Preview and summary slides use spaced repetition. Asking the audience questions, encouraging them to ask you questions, showing an outline of the topic, all are effective. Don't preview or summarize more than two or three slides. A preview slide that lists the title of the next 6 or 7 slides is overkill. Don't summarize the identical slides you previewed, it seems insulting.

Sounds

Insert relevant or humorous sounds. See the concept map below.

Involving the sense of hearing provides more sorting handles for linking the important points. Using multimedia involves more of the brain.

As the concept map shows below, **inserting** sounds will **not** mean they play in PPT. Sound files placed on a slide by the Insert menu choices must be in the same folder as the PPT show itself, or they won't play. The other way to make sounds play reliably is embed them in graphic objects.

One of the best internet sites for downloading sound effects is the website www.findsounds.com.

Embed the sounds by custom animating a graphic and in the task pane. Embed the sound under Effect Options; change No Sounds to Other Sounds... and point to the closed sound file.

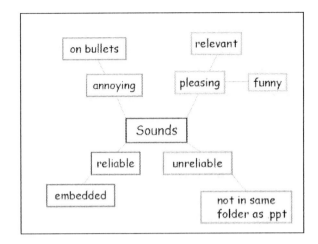

Rehearse

Once a bright student did not rehearse her term project in Powerpoint©. She did not test it on the instructor's computer with the projector connected. She did not buy a set of $2 head phones or borrow a set. When it was her turn to present to the class of 45 students, she found she had tied the sound of screeching car brakes to every element of every slide, because she did it to the Slide Master's Bulleted List Box. She had to scream to be heard over her own sound- what a fiasco. Doubtlessly, she realizes today that the word "rehearse" begins with "rehear."

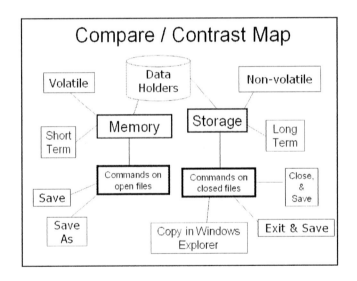

Using Open Office 2.0 Impress

First go to www.OpenOffice.org and download both the Open Office 2.0 and the JRE Java Runtime Environment software. Install the software per directions then reboot the computer for the changes to take place. Open the program Impress, which does what Power Point does- display ideas in a show business type format like a Broadway production. It's **free** to students and educators. Powerpoint by itself costs $130 or $250 if bundled with MS Office.

On starting Impress, our initial view shows 3 panes. Click on the Normal tab. In the middle window select the tab heading "Outline."

This Outline view is greatly magnified. We can zoom outward to see more text smaller, or zoom in to see less text but made larger. Use Control + the mouse wheel to zoom to a comfortable setting.

When we type in Outline tab heading, we create slides of text faster than by typing onto individual slides in placeholders. As a user types in the Outline tab heading, the very same words are appearing as slide titles and bulleted text.

In older versions of Impress (before version 2.0 came out) the main editing view was called Drawing View and it was the only view that could Insert, Slides. Now there is a toolbar button on the upper right, always visible.

For high speed text entry memorize and use the following keyboard commands for OUTLINE VIEW.

1. To get a new line of any indentation level hit Enter. New lines always match the formatting of the line above.

2. To demote a New Slide Title to Bulleted text (to move it right) hit the Tab key once.

3. To promote a Bulleted text item (to move it left) hold the Shift key down and strike the Tab key once. Shift + Tab reverses the Tab key used alone.

4. One trouble shooting tip is all that is missing. To fix a place where text does not look as we wish, place the cursor at the beginning of that formatting mistake and hit the Backspace key to merge it until it joins the text above. Next hit the Enter key to break the two lines apart again. Now tab or shift + tab will work correctly.

The next screen print shows what to type for slides 1 through 4 using Open Office Impress instead of Power Point. The step by step directions are in this Presentation Design textbook. Use the same text entry steps as the directions for doing it in PowerPoint on pages 16-18 approximately.

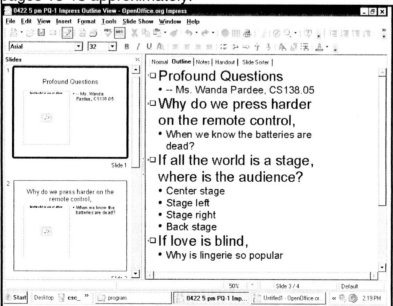

The directions about page 18 or so read like this: "Type Profound Questions, hit the Enter key, hit the tab key once, and type your name and class section. Hit Enter to get a new line then hold shift down while striking the Tab key to promote the newly added line to a new slide's title. Those specifics are about pages 16-18 in the textbook. One may automate the process by using Control + F to start the Find utility and typing the search phrase to read "Type Profound."

CLICK the menu choices VIEW, then SLIDE SORTER. Here are 8 operations you can do in VIEW, SLIDE SORTER in Open Office Impress:

1) Set the number of slides visible in the toolbar button area to 2 then to 3 then to 12. This is equivalent to a Zoom feature.
2) Right click any slide then choose CUT.
3) Right click on any remaining slide. A vertical blinking line appears. Choose PASTE. The new slide would follow in order. We could have drug the slide around instead.
4) Drag any slide except the title slide to a new position.
5) IF (but we don't right now) want to delete a slide we click once to select it then hit the DELETE key on the keyboard upper right.
6) IF we wanted a new slide we would click menu choices INSERT, SLIDE. Try this now. If we select a slide first the new slide goes in behind the selected slide. With nothing selected the newest slide appears as the last slide.
7) To reverse the last action above use Control + Z for UNDO last command. Try this step now.
8) To edit a slide we would DOUBLE CLICK it in Slide Sorter View. Try this now. It switches us to NORMAL VIEW for editing.

Slide Sorter View in Open Office Impress

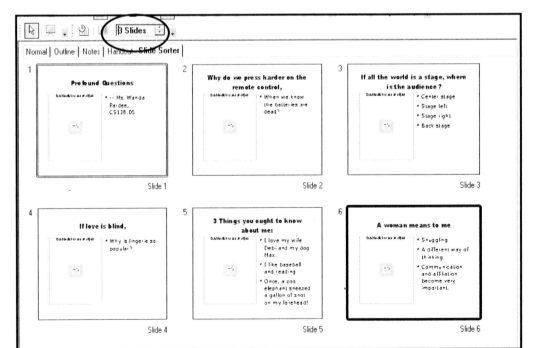

While in Slide Sorter view we double click on slide 5 to edit it in Normal View. **To insert a relevant graphic** start a Web Browser (Mozilla, Firefox, Netscape). Go to the **Google.com** home page and click above the text entry block, where it says "**Images**."

Type in "remote control." Look for an image with high contrast then right click that image and choose Copy.

Switch to Impress (by OpenOffice.Org). Paste the photo of a remote controller. The screen print below shows the slide as it exists at this point. Obviously it needs its text box reshaped. The slide is not balanced.

The next screen print has the bulleted text box selected for editing. The slanted lines around the edge have little embedded squares. These 8 points are called resizing handles. **Place the mouse pointer on the center resizing handle of the bottom border.** When it changes from a pointer to a 2-sided arrow, drag it upward. Finally, hit the escape key. Use muse dragging or better yet use the arrow keys to center it vertically on the slide. **Do similar steps on all slides to reshape the textboxes.** Wait until graphics have been placed on each slide.

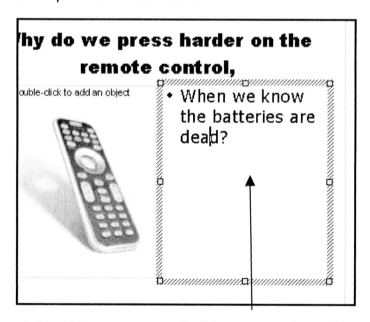

After we even out the white space on all slides we need to add custom animation to all slides. Click the menu choices **Slide Show, Custom Animation.**

The similarity of Impress to Powerpoint is so close that anyone who used Power point can figure out what to do in Impress 2.0 very quickly. For instance, one slide has four bullets which appear all at once.

There are two possibilities for causes. When the text place holder was selected it might have been selected **all** (showing green resizing handles). We could remove the animation and reattach it only after we see our cursor blinking inside the bulleted list box (the box would have slanted lines as its border). That did not work.

In Impress 2.0 we **double click the effect in the Task Pane** on the right. In Power point we would have clicked a down arrow list box to the right side of the listed effect then selected "Effect Options." Impress only requires us to double click the effect name instead.

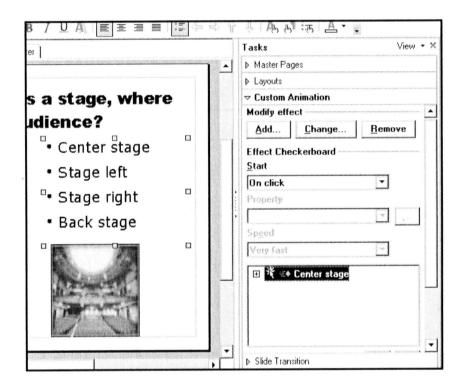

That brought up the Effect Options dialog box below:

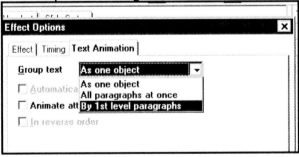

We designed the **text animation** tab to group **by first level paragraphs**. That makes first indentation level bullets appear one at a time instead of all at once. Why is this better? It chunks the material into smaller pieces that are easier to learn. It prevents a cluttered slide. If we show all bullets at once the audience will read different bullets than we talk about. Add it up.

Since we are animating the text it won't appear before we click a mouse button or hit the space bar. Unanimated objects precede animated objects.

Photos should appear before text bullets. Here is why. While the audience is reading text they are trying to picture in their minds what the words mean. Providing that picture to them first, speeds the learning process. If we animate photos we arrange them first on the list in the task pane. Unanimated photos and images appear before any animated images – before any mouse click. A hard to understand slide show is also boring.

Text should never move across the screen or monitor. Moving text is hard to read and quickly bores the audience. This is one of the most common complaints about slide shows – moving text.

The custom animations listed under **Basic category** are nearly all **excellent for text.** Never use the Fly In, Fly in Slow, or the Random Effects custom animations. The first moves. The second moves and moves too slowly at that, while Random Effects will violate all the rules of smart presentation design and do so unpredictably.

Text must be revealed either Very Fast or Fast, not medium, not slower than medium. An effect like diamond does not move across the screen; however its default speed is Medium. Until we make all animations Very Fast, Diamond would not be a good choice.

Audience surveys prove slow animation is boring.

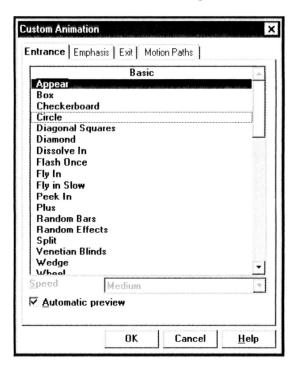

Wipe: One animation effect under the BASIC category is called **Wipe**. Its default appearance is to start at the bottom and wipe upward. For text it should be changed to **Wipe From the Left**. Then it appears as if coming from a high speed printer. An interesting property of the Wipe effect is **when applied to a line or an arrow** it looks as if an invisible hand is drawing it in real time. Kewl!

Animating text boxes differently on each slide may consume excess time. In a harsh workplace, click menu choices **View, Master, Slide Master** and apply custom animation to the master slide. Then don't add it to individual slides.

Notice at this point since a handful of task panes have been opened each previous one is listed as a one line entry in Impress 2.0. When a previous pane is selected from this list its pane expands and all other choices move to the bottom of the window. Also note the various views are selectable either from the Views menu or from Tab Headings in the center window pane.

Color in Open Office Impress

After inserting graphics, balancing extra white space and custom animating bulleted text, we next consider **color**. After watching 3,000 term project presentations over the past 5 years, it is apparent that most students choose color only because they like or dislike certain colors. Some continue selecting for the same personal reasons even when their color choices make it impossible to read the text! Unless the audience can read all the text, all the time spent on a slide show is wasted!

What makes slides legible? Choices for font, white space, graphics, animation effects, color and fill effects. Some were covered in previous chapters. We will explain next color contrast, including how to recognize and avoid medium shades. Then we apply high contrast to font and fill effects choices, and show some good and some awful examples.

Color Contrast

Three color choices to make are the text or font color, the slide background color, and sometimes the place holder's fill color. **Contrast is the difference in brightness between the font color and its background or fills color.**

Presentation software starts us with the highest color contrast possible: black on white. Only white font on a black background has equal legibility (contrast). White letters on a black background can look so artistic ("kewl") when refined by university students! Fonts like **Chiller, Fiesta,** and **Bernhard Fashion BT** can enhance good slide shows to like Broadway levels. Most students don't believe they can find emotionally satisfying color schemes within a range of colors first chosen for contrast (legibility) reasons. But they do.

Menu Choices

The immediate color behind the text is known as the Fill Color of its Placeholder. It has to be extremely light to contrast with black font.

High Contrast:

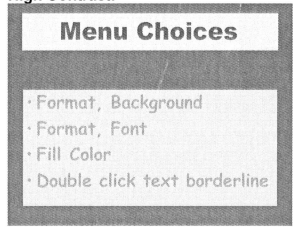

Medium Shades Low Contrast:

130

The slide Title on the left has very dark green font in the title and very light green Fill Color. The bulleted text box has a dark red font on a pale pink Fill Color. The slide background is very dark blue. The Font and the Fill Colors are polar opposites in light reflected, so the contrast on the left is excellent.

The slide colors on the right were all chosen because they were medium, halfway between dark and light. It lacks high contrast. **Audiences are bored by hard-to-read text.** To see the color palette (the "Magic Color Wheel") click the menu choices on the slide above then pick **More Colors..."**

The three menu choices listed above are not sufficient. To see color choices organized by shades from lightest to darkest, the next dialog box offers two pathways to selecting a color. It shows rectangular blocks with a few of the last colors we picked. These samples are not organized by light and dark so it is best to skip the rectangular patches.

High Contrast: **Dark on dark no contrast:**

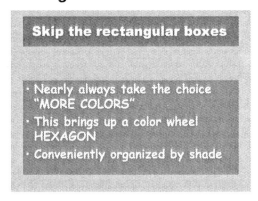   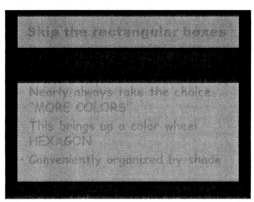

Underneath those colors is the choice, **"More Colors." Click that choice to see all colors on a hexagon arranged from very light in the center to very dark on the outside.** This is how we decide what is medium so we can avoid it..

High Contrast: Wrong Fill Effect Gradient on Background

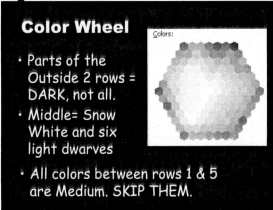   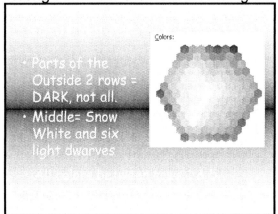

Please read the slide above before continuing.

Light colors defined and applied to Fill Effects

Light Colors are only the ones actually touching "Snow White" in the center.

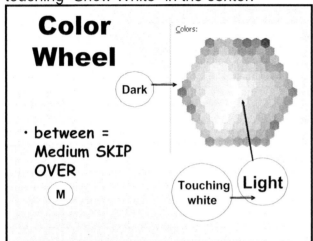

Snow White and the Six Dwarves totals 7 light colors. Only those 7 are "Light." This is the author's definition.

Here's where the choice to add Fill Effects appears after Format, Background.

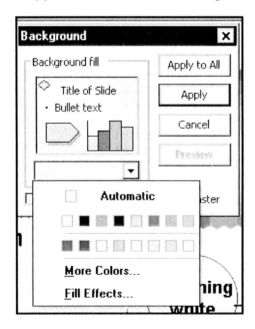

Fill Effects- a choice under More Colors

The illustration to the left has a gradient shaded background. To choose Format, Background we click the drop down list box arrow head. (Below)

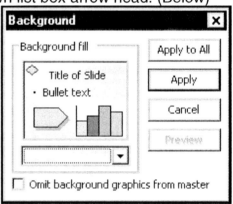

We chose a One Color Fill using for Color 1 a very light green (touching Snow White of course). We shaded it toward Light Fill not Dark.

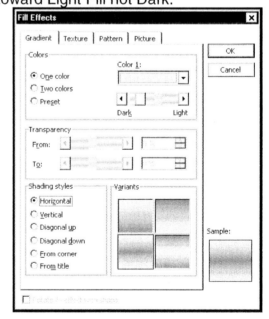

The default setting in MS Powerpoint was shown in the last table figure on the right. It is a serious blunder. The **default for the fill color** of a light color (color 1) is very dark set by MS designers. It should be Light not Dark.

The default choice will create dark and light streaks on the same slide background! Dark font will be unreadable in the dark area while light font will be unreadable in the light area.

The cure is to know to drag the slider bar to the Light side when the solitary color is light and the opposite side for a dark color. Then one color of font will be readable anywhere on that slide. And the key to the cure is knowing which areas of the "More Colors" hexagon have light and dark colors. Unless the designer sticks to extremes of light and dark it is not possible to explain why some choices are hard to read and bore the audience.

One Color, Dark Blue when shaded with black allows white text to be read at the back of a conference room. There are no unreadable patches.

The Fill Effects Gradient tab for a single, very dark color should be dragged toward "Dark" on the left side.

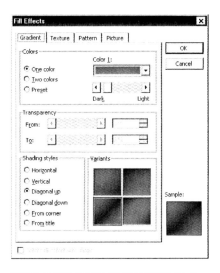

Another choice on the Fill Effects dialog box is Two colors. The choice to make is simple. Both colors for the gradient background should be very dark or both should be very light.

The rule for two-color gradients amounts to the rule for one-color:

Don't mix dark and light streaks on a slide background or we'll bore the audience.

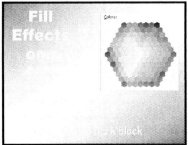

Choosing the Fill Effects Gradient tab's two color option with one color dark and one color light produces pretty stripes but an unreadable slide (on the left).

It is only a short time before the audience gets bored and quits trying to read along.

Immediate Feedback on Open Book Test 1

1. Control + Z reverses the last command.
2. 16 reversals.
3. You can NOT cancel File, Save and File, Print.
4. Which hand should you use for keyboard shortcuts? Both left and right
5. When you click in a text placeholder it is selected: Slanted border lines
6. Click and "Escape key" select with Checkered border lines
7. The best MS Design Template© to use is: Don't use a MS Design Template©.
8. On the first rectangular array of color choices, click on "More Colors…" under the rectangular choices
9. On the hexagonal color wheel, where can you find the following,?
   - a Dark color – outermost two rows from the center
   - a Light color – the first ring around the center white one
   - a Medium color – everywhere else (skip over medium shades)
10. Medium shades should never be used **Inside** a text box
11. The default (automatic) FILL COLOR in PPT text placeholders is __. None (transparent)
12. Control + T is the keyboard shortcut for formatting the font in a text placeholder.
13. Shadow effect makes text hard to read so avoid it.
14. For adding border lines around text placeholders double click its border.
15. Format, Background will change the color of one whole slide's background?
16. Double click the text placeholder border changes the fill color in a text placeholder?
17. List 5 readability choices
    - Wide spacing between letters (true type fonts)
    - Sans serif
    - Extreme color CONTRAST font with background or fill color
    - At least 28 points in size
    - No special effects except color of font; maybe bold.
18. **Sometimes** boldfacing a font make it more legible.
19. Do we need headings/titles on slides? (yes)   20. On all? (yes)

Immediate feedback on Open Book Test 2

1) Information organizer
2) Describe contents.
3) Continue the sentence in bullet one.
4) The third feature is Hyperlinking.
5) (T/F) False- Headings should be more noticeable somehow.
6) (T/F) False- Titles can be in different spots on different slides.
7) (T/F) False- 36-pooint Comic Sans MS is bigger than 36-point Times New Roman.
8) A title should be: (c) descriptive

9) A title serves as a one-slide (a) organizer.
10) When a title placeholder is selected All, for moving or changing all the contents at once, what is the border like? (b) Checkered lines
11) If title text is highlighted or selected, and we hold the Control Key while striking several times on the right (]) square parenthesis key (just above the E in the Enter Key) what happens? (d) it grows
12) Shift and the F3 (function 3) key cycles through 3 types of case. Which three? **all caps; all lowercase; and sentence case**
13) **Title** case capitalizes every major word but not articles (a, an, or the) nor short prepositions.
14) Change it on the Slide Master.
15) (T/F) ALL CAPS IS A GOOD CHOICE FOR TITLES = False
16) (T/F) Title Placeholders should never be animated except possibly on the first Title Slide? True
17) Custom animation should be used on all (b) bullets.
18) What is the shortcut to Center a title? Control + E.
19) Title placeholders by default, are centered horizontally and vertically which means as a new title line appears, text scrolls up not down. How do we fix that to scroll down? Format, Placeholder, Alignment tab heading, TOP not centered.

Immediate feedback Open Book Test 3

1) Which option gives more control over animations: Custom Animation does
2) It is optional whether to type in the title placeholder. (false)
3) What are two advantages to animating bulleted lists? Avoids clutter; chunks material into manageable bites.
4) You should embed sounds in a bulleted list (False)
5) What is the "First rule of software"? Show it where before we tell it what to do.
6) Which speed should you use (slow / medium / fast / very fast?) to animate bulleted text.
7) To animate a bulleted list box, what selection pattern should the list box border show, slanted lines or checkered?
8) Select one best animation for bulleted text from only these 4 choices: d. Very Fast, circle
9) False - Pinwheel or Swivel effect will turn your audience against your topic.
10) Only effects listed under Basic should go with text. (True)
11) Any effect listed under Basic should go with text. (False)
12) Text should randomly fly in (False)
13) Which effect makes lines and arrows appear to be drawn by an invisible hand? (Wipe)
14) (False)).
15) Bulleted text should always be animated, with a fast or very fast speed, and from the Basic category. (very true)
16) (False) Photographs should appear before not after bulleted text.
17) Title placeholders are optional and should be animated fast or very fast. (False on both accounts)
18) The technology used in a slide show should be remembered after the words are long forgotten. (False – the message should be remembered; the technology invisible
19) It is fine for all bullets to appear at once. (False)

20) If all bullets appear at once then one should look under Effect Options, but which tab heading? (Text)
21) End immediate feedback 3- animation design

More Questions

What is Rule 1 of all software programs?
(Show it where before we can tell it what to do. If a menu command is grayed out or dimmed out, showing we can't do it, it's usually because no object was selected first.)

Why animate bulleted lists?
(prevents visual clutter & cognitive (memory) overload

(T/F) Animated bullets gain attention and focus it. (true)

When sequence is important within a list, bulleted lists can be __?
(numbered.)

Custom Animation is which of the following?
a. entertainment
b. a cognitive tool
c. all of the above   (answer)